16

Studio Scripts

Series editor: David Self

Working

City Life

Communities

Situation Comedy

City Life

Edited by David Self

STUDIO SCRIPTS

Hutchinson
London   Melbourne   Sydney   Auckland   Johannesburg

Hutchinson & Co. (Publishers) Ltd
An imprint of the Hutchinson Publishing Group
24 Highbury Crescent, London N5 1RX

Hutchinson Group (Australia) Pty Ltd
30-32 Cremorne Street, Richmond South, Victoria 3121
PO Box 151, Broadway, New South Wales 2007

Hutchinson Group (NZ) Ltd
32-34 View Road, PO Box 40-086, Glenfield, Auckland 10

Hutchinson Group (SA) (Pty) Ltd
PO Box 337, Bergvlei 2012, South Africa

First published 1980

Introduction and notes © David Self 1980
Set in VariTyper Century Schoolbook

Printed in Great Britain by The Anchor Press Ltd
and bound by Wm Brendon & Son Ltd
both of Tiptree, Essex

British Library Cataloguing in Publication Data

City life. — (Studio scripts; 2).
  1. Children's plays, English
  2. English drama - 20th century
  I. Self, David II. Series
  822'.9'1408   PN6120.A4

ISBN 0 09 141081 9

Contents

Introduction

'Sir, when a man is tired of London, he is tired of life; for there is in London all that life can afford.' So said Dr Samuel Johnson in 1777, believing that London provided everything that was interesting, informative and desirable. Many have agreed with him, thinking that cities offer excitement, entertainment and fun. A city is, in the current slang, 'where it's all at, where you've got to be'.

Many would disagree, believing that city life is hard, depressing and cruel. A number of modern writers have taken this view, including, for example, D. H. Lawrence in his poem 'City Life':

When I am in a great city, I know that I despair.
I know there is no hope for us, death waits, it is useless to care.
For of the poor people, that are flesh of my flesh,
I, that am flesh of their flesh,
When I see the iron hooked into their faces
Their poor, their fearful faces
I scream in my soul, for I know I cannot
Take the iron hook out of their faces, that makes them so drawn,
Nor cut the invisible wires of steel that pull them back and forth, to work,
Back and forth to work.
Like fearful and corpse-like fishes hooked and being played

By some malignant fisherman on an unseen shore
Where he does not choose to land them yet, hooked fishes of
  the factory world.

Just as D. H. Lawrence feels pity for city-dwellers, trapped in their environment, so too do the three playwrights represented in this collection of television plays.

Lies

The central character of Willy Russell's play is fifteen-year-old Sammy Stubbs. Since his father left home, Sammy has assumed responsibility for his mother and younger brother, Terry. Sammy struggles to keep his mother off tranquillizers and Terry from smoking, and all the time dreams of being able to take the family away from Liverpool to a new life in Cornwall. The one sin he commits is to play truant from school, using his time to earn a little cash for the family fund. He is prepared to do anything so long as it is honest – unlike a fellow truant, Rolo, who spends his days shop-lifting.

Events conspire against Sammy. He is let down by his family and by others on whom he has relied, and (in a moment of despair) he steals a car and he and Rolo drive off towards Cornwall. After a visit to a motorway service station, however, his real character reasserts itself and he realizes that Cornwall is just a dream, a lie, and he drives back north to the harsh truths of everyday life.

Unlike Sammy, this author has found an escape in his writing. Willy Russell also admits to dreaming of escaping literally, of buying land and of living and writing in the country.

But Liverpool still holds him, even if it is on a longer noose than that with which it traps many of its

children. 'Liverpool *is* dirty, filthy, depressed; there is
the most acute pain around the place, but it is very
important to me: I'm secure there,' he says.

In *Lies* he presents not so much the security as the
pain. Sammy is a likeable, moral, hard-working,
intelligent boy. With the exception of his truancy, he
tries desperately hard to do the right thing – and is
bitterly hurt for his efforts. When the pain becomes too
much, he tries to run away but (because he is intelligent)
he knows there is no escape, there can be no more 'lies',
'the iron hook' of D. H. Lawrence's poem cannot be
removed, and he is trapped, 'hooked and being played
by some malignant fisherman on an unseen shore'.

The way in which fate treats Sammy so tragically
might be unconvincing were it not for the characteriza-
tion and the realistic and economic dialogue. At the
time of filming, boy actors (Steven McManaman, Mark
Moraghan and David Bradshaw) were full of
admiration for the realism of Russell's writing and fell
easily into the rhythms of the script. As the producer,
Andrée Molyneux, said, 'There is no doubt he's got an
ear for dialogue, but what he can also do is to present
kids so that you see the inside of them, their aspirations,
and you're caught by it all and you love them.'

Even if Willy Russell has a bleak view of city life, in
his eyes the people who live there, like young Sammy,
are still admirable and noble characters.

Uncle Sangi

Just as noble is the Sikh family in *Uncle Sangi* by Tom
Hadaway. Mr Dev, his wife and their son Sharm live
reasonably peacefully on Tyneside, where Mr Dev, an
educated man, runs a grocer's shop. Like Sammy in
Lies, he knows that life could be better, but (also like
Sammy) he works hard in the hope of improving his

way of life. Sharm meanwhile rejects at least some of the customs and virtues of Sikhism.

Into this situation comes Mr Dev's brother, Uncle Sangi. Unlike Mr Dev (who is much concerned with being thought 'honourable' and therefore is extremely law-abiding), Uncle Sangi is the 'black sheep' of the family, and also an illegal immigrant; he has entered Britain without permission and without proper papers. If discovered, he would be deported. Those who shelter him would also be guilty and 'dishonoured': certainly Mr Dev's business would be ruined.

Nevertheless the Devs allow him to stay for a short while, and though Sangi stays indoors most of the time he does go out a little – including a walk with Sharm. During this walk we hear something of Uncle Sangi's past and Sharm learns that occasionally hard decisions must be taken.

One evening when Mr and Mrs Dev have gone to see an Asian film at a local cinema, Sharm is involved in a row with a racist neighbour, during which the neighbour kicks Sharm's dog and is then bitten by it. The whole incident has been secretly witnessed by Uncle Sangi. The neighbour informs the police and Mr Dev anticipates any court case by deciding that the dog will be put down.

Having overheard his father's decision, Sharm is naturally heart-broken and wants his uncle to come forward to prove the dog's innocence. To do so is impossible as it would mean giving himself away. Not having been told the truth about his uncle, Sharm fails to understand his uncle's attitude.

However the boy takes matters into his hands: he steals Uncle Sangi's pistol and, taking his dog with him, goes to a dockland area and kills the dog himself – acting out a story that Uncle Sangi has told him earlier.

In this way a form of justice has been brought about, but presumably the tragic course of events will not end there. A taxi-driver has summoned the police to the scene where Sharm has shot his dog and where Sangi was hoping to prevent him from taking that action.

'Justice' is a recurring theme of the play. Mr Dev wants justice for himself and his family, he wants the justice of being thought well of, and he wants to be accepted because he does the 'just' thing. Sharm has wanted justice for himself and his dog. Sangi will meet justice because he has avoided it.

The family's problems occur because city life brings people into close proximity one with another. Mr Dev is on the one hand attempting to preserve his own culture – he and his wife go to Asian films and to the Sikh temple, the gurdwara; but he is also trying hard to conform to English ways.

Sharm is lonely and isolated precisely because he feels torn between the two cultures. This is therefore a dramatization of one of the most urgent problems in a multi-cultural society: how can different racial groups preserve their own dignity, traditions and customs, but at the same time blend into a united and harmonious community?

Uncle Sangi is a well-written and well-constructed play which explores these problems with courage and honesty. Hadaway's Sikh family is totally convincing; he makes no attempt to 'sell' them to a white audience by making them all honest heroes, nor does he try to pretend that 'foreigners are just like us really'. The family is Asian, and he recognizes that they *are* different; yet they share the environment of an English city. This play is a picture of what it is like to be in that situation, and will be as interesting and as instructive to Asian as to European viewers and readers.

Short Back and Sides

As in *Lies* and *Uncle Sangi*, this play shows us the
people who have to 'suffer' city life. But *Short Back and
Sides* is more centrally concerned with the town
planner who has created their environment.

John Hardy is the planning officer of a large
metropolitan county, and has been responsible for a
two-stage development plan that has demolished a
'traditional' inner city area and replaced it with urban
motorways, ring roads and an absence of anything
human, natural or neighbourly. We see Hardy taking
part in a local radio phone-in programme; we see him
with his teenage daughter (his wife has left him because
he was always so busy with his work); and then in a pub
and a barber's shop, both of which are in the middle of
an area that will suffer from the third stage of the great
development plan.

Gradually John Hardy comes to the conviction that
the plan has been a completely misguided idea, and he
admits this in another radio interview. He resigns from
his job, and is slightly surprised to find that this action
does not win any approval from the local people. Their
reaction is one of scorn that anyone should throw up
such a 'good' job. Nevertheless Hardy is happy in his
new-found freedom, and delights in re-discovering a
'natural' world in the company of his daughter.

Alan Plater has written that what television does best
is to examine reality:

Fairy-tales have little place on television: the most effective
television image is a close-up of a face – a refugee in India, a
miner on strike in South Yorkshire, a politician under the
studio lights, trying to shrug off an awkward question – faces
that are smiling, shouting, angry, desperate, embarrassed or
in repose.

It follows that television drama is built around the close-up, and generally around a small group of characters. We observe the changes in their relationship in close and precise detail; we see behind the eyes and read their thoughts.

Though he was not in this case writing about his own play, those words could well apply to *Short Back and Sides*. It is a frequently very funny play which explores a large problem through close-ups of a small group of people. Through their reactions, gestures and casual remarks, we appreciate the problems of their lives with developing sympathy and understanding. More than that though, we see ridiculed a planning system that has lost touch with the people it is planning for, and the horrors it can perpetrate in the name of progress.

Short Back and Sides is always entertaining. But because it is grounded in reality, it is also informative and thought-provoking and (like the other two plays in this collection) it raises a variety of questions about city life. Some of these points are included among the follow-up activities at the back of this book (page 143).

The Writers

Willy Russell
It might be said that Willy Russell romantically identifies with the young losers who people his plays. He himself left school at the age of 15, with an O-level in English language gained in the D stream of a secondary modern school. He then worked in the hair-dressing trade and at various unskilled jobs until he decided he wanted to teach. He worked for O- and A-levels which, in 1970, gained him a place at a teacher-training college in Liverpool.

Teaching lasted eighteen months ('It was enough') and by then his stage successes allowed him to take up writing full time. Even so, he normally writes only when commissioned. 'I suppose like a lot of people from the same background as me, I don't have the confidence to think that any idea I have will automatically find a buyer.'

His other plays include *Our Day Out* (in the anthology *Act One*) and *Terraces*, both published by Hutchinson.

Tom Hadaway
A Tynesider, Tom Hadaway is both a fishmonger (in North Shields) and a playwright. He writes frequently about the fish quay communities of the Tyne – as, for

example, in *The Filleting Machine*. This uncompromising but sympathetic picture of the problems of an ailing industry has been successfully produced on stage, on radio and television, and is published by Hutchinson in *Act Three*. Other plays and stories by Hadaway have been shown on BBC Television, and several of his plays have been produced in the north-east by The Live Theatre group.

Alan Plater

Born on Tyneside in 1935, Alan Plater grew up in Hull but returned to Newcastle upon Tyne to study architecture. He worked in an architect's office for two years, but then branched out on his own – working from home. This gave him time for writing, and his first radio play was broadcast in 1961.

Since then he has written many radio plays and was, for several years, the editor of *The Northern Drift*, a radio series which has given many young writers their first opportunity to hear their work broadcast.

Alan Plater has also written many television scripts – both original plays like *Short Back and Sides* and *Annie Kenney* (in *Act Three*, published by Hutchinson), and also episodes in such series as *Z Cars* and *Softly Softly*. He has also written for the cinema and for the theatre, where perhaps his greatest success has been the documentary play about coal-mining, *Close the Coalhouse Door*.

Television Drama and Its Audience

Certainly the most important fact about the audience for television drama is its size. When a Shakespeare play is transmitted, more people see it in that single evening than did in Shakespeare's whole life time. No wonder then that modern dramatists, like Dennis Potter, see television drama as an important medium:

There in the middle of the news bulletins, the ads, the sports, entertainments and party politicals, there in virtually every home in the land, seen with the social guard down and the texture of the modern world all around it, is a precious space for *drama*: the great playwrights of the past would surely have sought to use this medium to address their fellow citizens.

This points to one of the attractions of the television play. It allows the writer the chance to present his 'message' to an enormous audience in a way that is quite impossible in the theatre. Because of this and because (as we have seen) television is most successful when examining reality, the television plays which have had the greatest impact on their audiences have been those which have alerted them to new or forgotten truths or problems.

In their different ways, the three plays in this collection are primarily concerned with presenting different truths and alerting audiences to other people's problems.

Whether they are successful must be judged by the viewer (or the reader of this volume). Dennis Potter is aware that the impact of a play can quickly fade, and that there is no real contact between the television play-wright and his audience:

A television play is but a small fancy in the endless flux, an anecdote of sorts stranded in the middle of a torrent that swirls together images made out of the world's idiocies. It has the short and uncelebrated life of a gnat in a cool dusk, and is more often than not never seen again, for the tapes are wiped for future use. There is no tension crackling back across the footlights from unseen audiences, little sense of expectation, no vivifying tradition of great work, and only the scantiest of evidence that the bulk of its 'viewers' (oh, passive noun!) consider it a finer or deeper experience than any other sort of moving picture.

(*Observer*, 27 April 1975)

The B B C and the I T V companies do know quite a bit about the reactions of their audiences however.

The B B C's audience research works on the simple principle that, if you want to know what people watch and what they think of the programmes they see, you ask them. The B B C conducts some 2500 interviews a day every day. The method they have used since 1939 is what is called a 'quota sample' of people, aged 15 or over, who are selected as representative of the population.

In addition, the B B C asks a panel of viewers, some 6000 at any one time, to send in their views about programmes they've seen. Each year some 2000 broadcasts are reviewed by panel members.

I T V's monitoring system is J I C T A R, or Joint Industry Committee for Television, Advertising,

Research. J I C T A R uses an electronic device called a setmeter attached to the TV sets in a representative panel of 2655 households, who are paid a small fee. The meter records when the set was turned on and which channel it was turned to. J I C T A R's Top Twenty reports sets in use, not who, if anyone, is actually watching.

The two systems are often presented to the outside world as in conflict because the audience-share figures are higher for the B B C from the B B C audience research than from J I C T A R. In fact they measure different things.

On average during the 1970s, we watched TV nearly 18 hours a week, some $2\frac{1}{2}$ hours a day. Children of 5 to 14 watched TV nearly $3\frac{1}{2}$ hours a day. The statistic of four million as an average audience for plays is of considerable interest, especially when compared with audiences for live theatre or the sales of a novel (where 10,000 copies of a hardback means the book is a best-seller).

One way to find out about the television audience is to conduct your own audience research in your school, college or neighbourhood.

Besides trying to find out which programme had the largest audience in a given week, you might try to discover which programme was most liked (which may not be the same thing).

Other questions you might ask include:

1   How many hours' television do you watch a week?

2   Do you plan your viewing in advance to fit in with other things, such as seeing friends, and going to the cinema?

3   Which channel do you watch most?

4 Which of the following types of programme do you like watching most?

News	Comedy series
Documentaries	Old films
Plays	Sports
Drama series	Other things

5 With the exception of the news, what is the single *best* programme or series you've ever seen?

6 What is the single *worst* programme or series you've ever seen?

7 Who is your favourite TV personality?

8 Can you remember any single play that you particularly liked?

9 Can you mention any single play that you feel has taught you something or has changed your mind about something?

10 How would you improve television?

Notes on Presentation

Even an informal classroom reading of a playscript is helped by rehearsal. Remember, not even the experienced professional actor is happy to sight-read, but usually prefers to have the chance to look over his part before a first reading in front of his colleagues. So, once a play has been cast, those who will be reading should be given the chance to look over their lines, make sure that they know when to pause; when to 'come in quickly' at the end of the previous speech; and to check that they appreciate the mood, etc., of their character at any given moment.

It is much easier to read to a class from the front of a traditional classroom, and from a standing position or a position where you can be seen by your audience. It may be useful to appoint a director who will decide the location of various settings and rehearse the actors in basic movements, checking that they know when and where to enter and exit.

Note that it is possible for a class to break up into groups, and for each group to rehearse its own interpretation of a play, and then for the groups to present their readings in turn to the whole class.

In preparing the scripts for inclusion in this book, I have modified some of the film and studio directions so that when the plays are being read aloud these directions (along with scene titles and descriptions of settings) can be read aloud by an 'announcer'. In a classroom presentation, it might be helpful if he or she were in view of the 'audience' but away from the acting area.

Note that provided these directions are read sympathetically, a television play will read as fluently in the classroom as will a radio or stage play; but it should not be forgotten that (like any good television play) it was conceived in visual terms, and it will be fruitful to discuss (as the original director must have done) where and how each scene should be 'shot' to realize the author's intention.

It will also be instructive to work out which scenes were recorded in a studio, and for which scenes it was necessary to go filming on location.

When presenting plays like these on stage (whether it be in a formal production or informally to just a small audience) thought must be given as to how they must be adapted and how their original pace can be maintained.

A distinguishing feature of television plays is that, unlike stage plays, they can make speedy transitions from one scene to another. They can also include scenes which actually involve travel (for example, scenes where characters walk along a street or travel by car).

These scripts will work successfully on stage, however, if they are given a stylized production either in the round or on an almost empty stage. Specially taken 35 mm slides, projected scenery or captions can announce locations to an audience, and the use of sound effects can be an effective substitute for scenery (especially in outdoor scenes such as those involving traffic). Other exterior scenes could be created entirely by the use of slides, taped voices and sound effects. Sound effects can also be used to suggest the presence of large crowds at meetings, etc. Costume and hand-held props can also do much to replace scenery. In indoor scenes, the use of stage furniture should be restricted so as to preserve fluency and speed of staging. Part of the success of any television play lies in the fact that it can cut from one scene to another; and, in a stage performance of a television play, lighting changes must be used to effect such 'jump-cuts' and to make us believe the acting area now represents a different location.

Even if you have seen the television production of any of the plays, resist the temptation merely to copy the screen version. Study the scripts and devise your own new productions.

Although all the plays in this series of volumes will stand on their own, double (and even triple) bills can be constructed to form an evening's entertainment – possibly with the different years in a school each presenting one play.

Acknowledgements

For permission to publish the plays in this volume, the editor and publishers are grateful to the following authors and their agents: Willy Russell and Margaret Ramsay Ltd for *Lies*; Tom Hadaway for *Uncle Sangi*; Alan Plater and Margaret Ramsay Ltd for *Short Back and Sides*. All applications to perform these plays, whether by amateurs or professionals, should be made to Margaret Ramsey Ltd, or, for *Uncle Sangi*, via the publisher.

We are also grateful for permission to use the photographs in this volume: *Lies* and *Uncle Sangi*, British Broadcasting Corporation; *Short Back and Sides*, photographs © Trident Television Ltd 1976.

Lies
Willy Russell

First broadcast in two parts by B B C School Television
in the series *Scene*

Characters
Sammy Stubbs, aged 15
Rolo, his friend
Terry Stubbs, Sammy's younger brother, aged 12 or 13
Mrs Stubbs, Sammy's mother, aged 35
Mr Moore, teacher
Mr Derbyshire
Store Manager
Store Detective
Boys in class
Motorists

Sammy (played by Stephen McManaman) and Mr Derbyshire (Hal Jeayes) in the BBC production of Lies

Part I

---

1 A road in the centre of Liverpool

We see city workers, shoppers and then two boys. They are walking aimlessly, occasionally looking in shop windows, pointing and then ambling on.

2 A classroom

*A teacher, **Mr Moore**, is taking the register. The pupils answer to their names. When the teacher gets to the name Stubbs, there is no answer. He looks up.*

Mr Moore: Sammy Stubbs?
First boy: He's saggin' again, sir.
Second boy: He's always saggin'.
Mr Moore: All right, all right!
Third boy: Saggin' Stubbs!

   [*Laughter from the class*]

3 A shopping centre

The two boys are looking at a shop window. There are various temptations to buy: adverts, special terms, etc.

Rolo: What would y' do if y' had a thousand quid?

Sammy: Take me ma an' our Terry an' go an' live in Cornwall.

Rolo: Would y'?

Sammy: [*Stopping outside a travel agent's and looking in*] Yeh.

Rolo: I'd get a car.

Sammy: [*Sees an advert for a Cornish holiday*] I'd buy a house in Cornwall.

Rolo: For a thousand quid? You'd need more than that.

Sammy: Not a perfect house, stupid, a derelict. Y' could get one for that price an' fix it up.

Rolo: You're ahead the ball you are. What the hell d' y' wanna live in Cornwall for? It's miles away, isn't it?

Sammy: It's three hundred an' forty four miles from here to Penzance. If y' wanna go to North Cornwall it's not as far.

Rolo: [*Looking at him*] You'll be on *Mastermind* next.

Sammy: Don't be daft, Rolo. All y' have t' do is look it up in a book of maps.

Rolo: An' what d' y' waste y' time doin' that for?

Sammy: I'm not wastin' me time, Rolo. I'm goin' there one day.

Rolo: [*Laughing*] You're nuts, you are, Sammy. I always said you were soft in the head.

Sammy: [*Walking away,* **Rolo** *following*] Is that what y' think, Rolo?

Rolo: You're ahead the ball. Is this all y' do when you're saggin', walk around town?

Sammy: Yeh.

Rolo: Don't y' go robbin' in the shops?

Sammy: [*Looking at him*] No! I just keep me eye out for an openin'. Y' can always find a chance if y' keep y' eyes open.

Rolo: A what?

Sammy: A chance, an openin'. Y' know, a bit of a job for the day, a chance t' make some money. I've done all sorts.

Rolo: Like what?

Sammy: All sorts: collectin' in the trolleys for the supermarket, dumpin' boxes an' that in the big stores. Do anythin', helpin' women carry the shoppin', they give y' tips if y' lucky . . . .

Rolo: An' that's how y' gonna make a thousand quid, is it? Helpin' women with their shoppin' bags. How much d' they give y', Sammy? Ten pence? [*Laughs*]

Sammy: Sometimes. Sometimes y' get more. A woman give me a quid once.

Rolo: [*Impressed*] What! Just for carryin' her bags?

Sammy: Yeh.

Rolo: [*Pause*] She must have fancied y'.

Sammy: Yeh, she must have done!

Rolo: [*Laughing*] You're a nutter, you're a looney!

Sammy: I know what I'm doin'. D' y' know what you're doin', Rolo?

Rolo: [*Puzzled*] Walkin' down the street.

Sammy: I'm gonna make it, Rolo. I'm gonna be big I am.

Rolo: Yeh, yeh.

Sammy: Just slowly. Gradually buildin' up all the

time, not too fast, just lookin' for me openin', for the main chance.

Rolo: Yeh . . . . King of the Shoppin' bag Carriers.

Sammy: [*Stopping*] Listen you – I didn't ask you to sag off with me, Rolo. If y' don't like the company y' can sod off back to school where y' really belong.

Rolo: [*Offended*] Ooer! What about you? You belong there as well.

Sammy: No way. I'm not gonna find me openin' sittin' in a classroom, am I?

4   Sammy's house: The lounge

The lounge is past its best. When first decorated and furnished, the room must have been done so with pride, but the pride has now gone. There is a feeling of resignation about the place. Sammy's mother is smoking and watching morning television. **Terry,** *Sammy's brother, is in pyjamas and also watching TV.*

Terry: Gis a ciggy, mam.

Mrs Stubbs: Y' too young to be smokin'.

Terry: Ah go on. [*Pause*] Y' let our Sammy smoke.

Mrs Stubbs: Sammy's fifteen. Anyway, he packed up last year.

Terry: [*Pause*] Well he was smokin' when he was twelve.

Mrs Stubbs: He wasn't.

Terry: He was, y' know.

Mrs Stubbs: [*Pause*] Anyway, Sammy never had asthma.

Terry: [*Pause as he tries to come up with a new*

approach] Go on . . . give us one. [*Pause*] Just one, mam. [*Pause*] Go on . . . just one.

Mrs Stubbs: [*Flings packet across*] Here! Take them, take the bloody lot!

Terry: [*Getting up and grabbing the packet*] I only want one.

Mrs Stubbs: You wait till Sammy gets in. I'll tell him, I'll tell him about you smokin'.

Terry: [*Considers this, looking at her. Decides it's worth the risk, takes out a cigarette and lights up*] D' y' want one of y' tablets?

Mrs Stubbs: No I don't wanna tablet.

Terry: I thought they made y' feel better. [*Pause*] You're in a nark, aren't y'?

Mrs Stubbs: [*Looks at* **Terry**] Agh. Give us one of them. It's just me. [*She lights the cigarette*] I'm thirty-five an' I feel more like sixty-five.

Terry: Are you thirty-five, mam? I thought y' were only about twenty-eight, somethin' like that.

Mrs Stubbs: It's this place. Livin' in this place ages y' before y' time.

Terry: Honest y' know . . . y' only look about twenty-eight. Y' look younger than that when y've got y' make-up on.

Mrs Stubbs: When I was twenty-eight . . . no, twenty, when I was twenty, y' should have seen me.

Terry: I'll bet y' were great, weren't y', mam?

Mrs Stubbs: The times I had. Y' should've seen me when I went to the clubs. They all knew me as well. I didn't need a membership card anywhere. All the doors were open to me. Do you know why, Terry?

Terry: Cos y' were a great dancer, weren't y', mam?

Mrs Stubbs: Dance! You should've seen me dancin' son. They didn't know what dancin' was all about till I got out there. [*Pause*] I was always dancin' when I was young.

Terry: Y' still could, mam. You'd be great.

Mrs Stubbs: It was your father who stopped me dancin'. They're all the same, men. They'll dance forever, when they're tryin' to get to know y'. But when they've got y', they never wanna dance with y' again.

Terry: You could still go dancin', mam. Why don't y' eh? Why don't y' go out with y' mates one night?

Mrs Stubbs: Yeh. Maybe I will. Me an' the girls. [*Pause*] Maybe I'll do that. When me nerves get better.

Terry: Oh yeh. I forgot about y' nerves.

[*A knock on the door*]

Mrs Stubbs: Go an' see who that is son. If it's anyone for money tell them we've got none.

[**Terry** *goes to the front door and opens it. The teacher,* **Mr Moore***, is standing there*]

Terry: [*Hiding his fag*] We sent a doctor's note in, sir. I've got asthma. [*Automatically coughs to prove it*]

Mr Moore: Is your mother in, Terry?

Terry: Come in. Mum, it's sir. It's Mr Moore.

[**Mrs Stubbs** *is trying to tidy the lounge.* **Terry** *and* **Mr Moore** *enter*]

Mr Moore: Hello, Mrs Stubbs, how are you?

Mrs Stubbs: Didn't y' get the doctor's note Mr Moore?

I sent one in, I did Mr Moore. He's terrible with the asthma, aren't y', Terry? [**Terry** *provides an obliging cough*]

Mr Moore: We got Terry's note from the doctor. Mind you I don't know what the doctor would have to say if he knew Terry was smoking!

Mrs Stubbs: Who? Terry? Smoking? Terry Stubbs, put that out this minute. God knows where he got that from, Mr Moore. Y' can't do a thing with them these days can y'. Mind you, it's you people I feel sorry for – yours must be an awful job. You've got my sympathy, you have.

Mr Moore: Mrs Stubbs. It's Sammy I've come about.

Mrs Stubbs: Oh!

5   The toy department of a large store

Sammy *and* **Rolo** *are strolling around.*

Rolo: [*Looking at a toy*] Oogh . . . look at that, Sammy, they're great them. I've seen them on the telly. I'd love one of them.

Sammy: What for?

Rolo: So's I could have one. It'd be great havin' one of them.

Sammy: But what good would it do y' to have one of them?

Rolo: [*Dumbfounded*] Don't be stupid. Y' could play with it.

Sammy: You're a jackdaw, you.

Rolo: Y' know what I'd love t' do, eh? I'd love to have an hour in here an' I could have everythin' I could carry.

Sammy: Junk.

Rolo: Go 'way. It's great. Like *Sale of the Century*. Know what I'd love eh, t' go on the *Generation Game*. Y' know at the end Sammy, y' know where all the prizes come down the conveyor belt, no one's ever remembered everythin' that was on it. I bet I could. I'd be great at that.

Sammy: What y' talkin' about? Can't you see it's just crap, eh? It's junk, this stuff. It makes y' happy for ten minutes an' then it's broken or pushed away in a drawer or under the stairs. Y' don't need stuff like this Rolo.

Rolo: [*Looking at him*] I do.

[*The Department* **Manager** *approaches them*]

Sammy: [*To* **Rolo**] This looks like the boss. I'll ask him.

Rolo: Ask him what?

Manager: [*Suspicious*] Can I help you?

Sammy: [*Formal*] Are you the manager of this department?

Manager: Yes?

Sammy: Ah, good morning, sir. [**Rolo** *is stifling laughter*] We were wondering if you had any temporary jobs?

Manager: What sort of jobs?

Sammy: Anything. Anything you need doing for an hour, half a day, a day . . . we don't mind what we do.

Manager: No. We don't employ casual labour.

Sammy: Well maybe you've . . . .

Manager: I said no!

Sammy: Oh. I see. Well . . . thanks for your time. Perhaps we'll call in again tomorrow in case there's a . . . .

Manager: We don't employ casual labour at all.

Sammy: Yes . . . but you don't know what tomorrow might bring do you? I mean you might . . . .

Manager: Would you mind leaving the premises?

Sammy: Well . . . thanks for seeing us. We're most grateful. [*He smiles and turns away,* **Rolo** *following.* **Manager** *stands and watches them go. When they are within safe reach of the escalator* **Rolo** *turns back to the* **Manager**]

Rolo: [*Shouting at him*] Y' soft dick head! [*He runs to the escalator*] Come on, Sammy. [**Sammy** *watches* **Rolo** *disappearing down the escalator.* **Sammy** *continues his unhurried pace.* **Rolo** *waits at the foot of the escalator for* **Sammy**] That showed him, didn't it, Sammy? Stuck up snob.

Sammy: [*Arriving at the foot of the escalator*] Why did you do that Rolo?

Rolo: Snob, wasn't he, eh?

Sammy: Listen, Rolo, y' never gonna get anywhere if y' behave like that. Fellers like him, they're in control, aren't they, they make the bleedin' decisions. It's no good just shoutin' at them, is it?

Rolo: I showed him, didn't I?

Sammy: Showed him what? All he's gonna do now is believe even more that he was right not t' give us a job. Why didn't y' just walk away all calm an' polite?

Rolo: Y' what? You're just a creeper you. Y' should've heard y'. [*Mimicking*] 'Good morning sir.' Soft git!

Someone like that, he'd never give a job to the likes of us.

Sammy: Look, soft nut. If we'd just kept walkin' dignified an' polite, then he wouldn't have been able to just write us off. All day he would've been thinkin' to himself, 'Was I right to do that? They were polite, they didn't argue.' It would've made him think, Rolo. We could've come in again tomorrow morning an' I'll bet he would've changed a bit.

Rolo: Who are you kiddin'?

6   Sammy's house

Mr Moore: I don't want to be an ogre, Mrs Stubbs, but every communication has been ignored.

Mrs Stubbs: I tell him, Mr Moore, honest to God I do, don't I, Terry? I say Sammy you've got to go to school. But he won't. [*Pause*] He says school's for kids.

Mr Moore: [*Exasperated*] But Sammy's only fifteen. He *is* a kid.

Mrs Stubbs: But y' can't say that to Sammy, Mr Moore. What's he like Terry, if anyone says he's a kid? See Mr Moore, it's since his dad left. Sammy sees himself as the head of the household. D' y' know what I mean?

Mr Moore: Yes, I do Mrs Stubbs, but the point is that in the eyes of the law, he is still a child and should be at school.

Mrs Stubbs: He's a good lad, y' know. He wouldn't do anything wrong.

Mr Moore: I'm not saying that he would Mrs Stubbs. But let me point out Mrs Stubbs, truancy often is the first step to someone going wrong.

Mrs Stubbs: No. Sammy wouldn't do anything wrong Mr Moore. He's sensible.

Mr Moore: Well if he's sensible, how come he's not turning up to school? I wouldn't mind so much if he was a no-hoper. But he could get a lot out of school. He's intelligent. If Sammy had stuck to it he'd be sitting O-levels now.

Mrs Stubbs: [*Pause*] I don't know. I just don't know. I can't walk him there, can I?

Mr Moore: [*Pause*] Well, Mrs Stubbs, I've done all I can. You realize that the next step has to be prosecution? If Sammy refuses point blank to come to school, then I'm afraid it's the only course left open to us.

7 The department store

Sammy *and* **Rolo** *are on the ground floor heading for the exit.* **Rolo** *suddenly notices something.*

Rolo: Oh . . . look at that. [*He points at a posh table lighter*]

Sammy: [*Stopping him*] Y' never listen you, do y'? It's garbage, that's all. Y' like a drug addict you aren't y'? Y' want somethin' t' make y' happy, then when that wears off y' want some more.

Rolo: [*Aggressively pulling away*] Well! What's it t' you?

8 Sammy's house: the hall

Mrs Stubbs *closes the front door.* **Mr Moore** *has just gone.*

Mrs Stubbs: Terry! Terry. [**Terry** *is watching television*] Where's me tablets? Have y' seen me tablets?

Terry: [*As she finds them*] I thought y' didn't wanna tablet.

9 A derelict warehouse

It has no doors, but does have windows and a large loading bay. **Sammy** *is looking around;* **Rolo** *is bored.*

Rolo: What we come in here for?

Sammy: [*He is miles away with his own thoughts*] What?

Rolo: Come on, let's go to the shops.

Sammy: What for? I don't wanna buy anythin'.

Rolo: I'm not talkin' about buyin'. I was thinkin' more about robbin'.

Sammy: [*Looks at* **Rolo** *and chooses to ignore him. He resumes looking around the warehouse*] Now see this place . . . it's wasted. Know what I'd do if I had this place? I'd turn it into a café . . . no, restaurant.

Rolo: [*Laughing*] An' feed all the rats? It's just a broken down dump. It's only a derelict.

Sammy: Yeh. It is to you, Rolo, but you're not seein' the potential, are y'?

Rolo: The what?

Sammy: The potential – that means what y' can do with it.

Rolo: I'll tell y' what y' can do with it. [*Laughs*] Come on. Let's go to the shops.

Sammy: I'd put me office over here. I'd be sort of, in the background, in charge but in the background. I'd put me mam in charge, out front. She'd love somethin' like that, y' know.

Rolo: She's all right your ma, isn't she? I've seen her. She's dead young lookin', isn't she?

Sammy: She *is* young.

Rolo: I wish my ma was young. She's ancient. My ma looks like other people's gran'mas. Moan! She never stops moanin', y' know. Nag, nag, nag all the time. No wonder me old feller hates her. They're never happy women, are they? Unless they've got half a dozen bottles of stout down them, they're all right then. But most of the time they're just moanin' machines.

Sammy: Yeh, an' who could blame them?

Rolo: I can. They don't have much to do, they stay home all day . . . .

Sammy: Oh yeh, they stay home all day! That's a great life that, isn't it? Would you stay home all day, every day?

Rolo: They go the shops don't they? They get out sometimes.

Sammy: [*Sarcastic*] Oh yeh. Great, that, isn't it!

Rolo: [*Scowling*] Come on, let's go.

Sammy: No wonder they moan, they were all girls once. An' what happens to them, eh? My ma's not gonna be like the rest of them. When I make it, she'll be someone, my old girl.

Rolo: All right, all right! [*Pause*] I wanna go the shops.

Sammy: Well go then. [*Goes to the loading bay and looks out over the adjacent car park*]

Rolo: I will! [*He doesn't. Pause*]

Sammy: Eh . . . look at that, Rolo.

Rolo: [*Looking at the car park and the queue of cars*] What?

Sammy: That, Rolo, is an openin'.

Rolo: [*Puzzled*] Just looks like a car park t' me.

Sammy: That's cos y' haven't got y' eyes open, Rolo. [*He exits*]

Rolo: I have.

10   The car park

A man in the queue of cars is standing on the running board of his car, craning to see if there are any free spaces on the far side of the park.

Sammy: [*Approaching him*] That's all right sir, you stay in the car, as soon as there's a place I'll let you know.

Man: Oh . . . thanks son, thanks a lot.

Sammy: You're welcome. [*A woman approaches the car park, taking her car keys from her bag*] I think there'll be one free in a second, sir. [*He waves out the woman's car and waves in the man's. He makes a great show of waving the driver into the space. The driver gets out and tips him*]

11   Inside the warehouse

Rolo *is standing in the doorway of the warehouse, watching* **Sammy** *who is over in the car park.* **Rolo** *laughs to himself as he watches* **Sammy**, *and then goes into the warehouse.* **Sammy** *returns from the car park and enters the warehouse.*

Rolo: Gonna make y' fortune at that, are y'?

Sammy: Listen, Rolo, that's only the start, finding spaces for them. Look, we build it from there, right? We provide a polishin' service, change for those who haven't got the right money for the meter, we could do all that.

Rolo: We?

Sammy: But look, it's a chance t' make a few bob, isn't it?

Rolo: 'Ey dimbo - if y' wanna make a few bob, y' don't do it like that. There's all kinds of shops in town an' y' can lift what y' like.

Sammy: If you wanna go on the rob, Rolo, y' on y' own. Y' don't get t' be anyone by robbin' stuff, that's for idiots.

Rolo: Yeh? We'll see who the idiot is, won't we? I'll see y' after.

Sammy: Don't come back here if y've been robbin'.

Rolo: Why? Don't be stupid, Sammy, the . . . .

Sammy: I've got t' go. There's a customer.

12   The car park

A car is pulling out. **Sammy** *goes across to it.*

Rolo: [*Shouting after him*] 'Ey Sammy, at least y've come up in the world from the day y' carried shoppin' bags. [*Laughs*]

13   The department store: the sweet counter

Rolo *looks around, grabs two bars of chocolate cream from the sweet counter, and slips them into his windcheater.*

14   The car park

Sammy *opens a car door for a woman driver. She smiles and opens her purse.*

15   The department store: the stationery counter

Rolo *slips a pen into his windcheater.*

16   The car park

Sammy *gets the elbow from a driver, who waves* **Sammy** *on his way.* **Sammy** *is philosophical about it, and waves to the next car to indicate that a space will soon be free.*

17   The kitchenware department of the store

Rolo *grasps a cheese grater, and moves quickly on.*

18   The warehouse

Sammy *is searching in his jacket pockets;* **Mr Derbyshire** *is standing in the doorway.* **Sammy** *finds the change he has been looking for, turns and gives it to* **Mr Derbyshire**.

Sammy: There y' go, sir. How's that?

Mr Derbyshire: [*As they exchange coins*] Many thanks. I'm very grateful, young man. I'm always doing it. The times I leave the house without checking that I've got change for the meter!

Sammy: Well it's easily done, isn't it, sir? It's a mistake anyone can make.

Mr Derbyshire: I suppose it is.

Sammy: But in future don't worry about it. Park here every day, do y', sir?

Mr Derbyshire: Most days.

Sammy: Well I'll always have change so don't worry. OK?

Mr Derbyshire: You're going to be here regularly, are you?

Sammy: Well there's a demand, isn't there? So if my services are required . . . why not?

Mr Derbyshire: Why not indeed!

Sammy: I just saw the gap. So I filled it.

Mr Derbyshire: You're an enterprising lad, aren't you? What's your name?

Sammy: Sammy Stubbs.

Mr Derbyshire: Well Sammy Stubbs, I'm very impressed, and it's not often that you'll hear me say that. You see, when you get into my position in life, you've seen most things.

Sammy: I'll be able to say that one day. This is only a start. But I'll make it, y' know, sir. I'll be someone important.

Mr Derbyshire: I can see I'll have to watch out. Is this town big enough for both of us?

Sammy: Not round here. I'm not stayin' here. As soon as I've got the money I'm goin' away with me mam an' our Terry.

Mr Derbyshire: And where are you going to?

Sammy: Cornwall.

Mr Derbyshire: Know it well. I've spent a lot of time in Cornwall. Torquay, places like that. [**Sammy** *looks at him*] And what will you do in Cornwall?

Sammy: I don't know yet. Some sort of business. Not

trash. Somethin' that people want, that's worth doin'. Boats, somethin' like that.

Mr Derbyshire: It's a hard world, the business world, Sammy. Take it from me.

Sammy: I know it's hard. But I'm gonna do it.

Mr Derbyshire: You've certainly got it all worked out, haven't you? I see I shall have to start charging you rent.

Sammy: [*Puzzled*] Eh?

Mr Derbyshire: [*Laughing*] Well, if you use premises you should pay for them, shouldn't you?

Sammy: What? This place? Do you own this place?

Mr Derbyshire: Well . . . the er . . . yes. My company does.

Sammy: [*Impressed*] Go 'way, I didn't know. I'll pay though. How much?

Mr Derbyshire: [*Laughing*] No, no. I was only joking. The company's not doing anything with this building at the moment.

Sammy: Listen, sir, y' know what you should do with it, you should turn it into something.

Mr Derbyshire: Should I? Well what would you do, Sammy?

Sammy: I'd . . . I'd make this place into a fantastic café, a restaurant.

Mr Derbyshire: [*Preparing to go*] Well we'll have to think about that, won't we?

Sammy: You do that, sir. You have a think about it. I'll tell y' somethin', you want someone to run it for y', I know exactly the right person.

Mr Derbyshire: Do you? Well. I must get going.

Very busy day today.

Sammy: Tarar. 'Ey, what's y' name sir?

Mr Derbyshire: Derbyshire. W. D. Derbyshire.

Sammy: W. D. Derbyshire. All right, Mr D, don't worry now. I'll look after the car for y'. [*Watches in admiration as* **Mr Derbyshire** *goes*]

19 The warehouse

Rolo *enters and greets* **Sammy**.

Rolo: Wait'll y' see what I've got, Sammy!

Sammy: I don't want you bringing robbed stuff here.

Rolo: Oh go 'way. Look. [*Opens his jacket and a whole variety of goods spill out*]

Sammy: Listen, I said . . . .

Rolo: [*Excited*] Look!

Sammy: That's nothin' – that's trash – look what I made today. [*Shows him some money*]

20 Sammy's house

Mrs Stubbs *is sitting at the kitchen table drinking tea. We hear the front door open and close and then* **Sammy** *enters the kitchen. He is excited and cheerful.*

Sammy: [*Making a fanfare sound*] We're on our way, mam.

Mrs Stubbs: There isn't much for tea, Sammy.

Sammy: We're *going*! Know how much I earned today?

Mrs Stubbs: There's tea in the pot.

Sammy: [*Getting a cup*] I met this feller today, mam,

a really important feller, y' know, really classy, good suit an' that, no junk.

Mrs Stubbs: Mr Moore came this morning.

Sammy: Ah, forget him. No, this feller . . . .

Terry: [*Appearing in the doorway*] Hi Sammy.

Sammy: All right, Terry? W. D. Derbyshire his name is. He's opening a new restaurant and guess who's gonna be workin' there?

Mrs Stubbs: You've got to go to school, Sammy.

Terry: Or y'll have t' go t' court, he said.

Sammy: Ah forget that. Listen, he's gonna put me in charge – when it's built like – I mean, look a year doin' somethin' like that, we'd soon have enough to move t' Cornwall.

Mrs Stubbs: Sammy! You've got to go to school.

Sammy: What y' goin' on about school for? I'm talkin' about Cornwall, mam. I'm talkin' about goin' there. Listen, it's no rubbish, just give us a year in Mr Derbyshire's café an' we'll be on our way.

Mrs Stubbs: Huh. Y' couldn't ask him for y' wages in advance could y'? An' we'll go now.

Sammy: [*Laughing*] A year's not long, mam.

Mrs Stubbs: It is when y've got to out and work at *that* place every night.

Sammy: Don't go tonight, mam. Have a night off.

Mrs Stubbs: [*Getting up to get ready for work*] Y' don't get paid if y' don't go in, Sammy.

Sammy: You can afford a night off. Go on. Look, I made a fiver today.

Terry: Go on, stay home tonight, mam.

Sammy: Yeh. Go on. I'll tell y' all about Cornwall. I'll get the maps out an' show y' where we're gonna go.

Terry: Near the sea.

Sammy: We'll be able to hear the waves at the bottom of the garden. It'll be sunny down there, the air's cleaner an' it's near the gulf stream. We'll get there y' know. I'll make sure of that. Y' won't need to look at y' tablets when we get down there. He won't know what the word asthma means when he gets his lungs full of that Cornish air. You leave it to me. I won't let y' down.

Terry: Y' can go surf riding in Cornwall, can't y', Sammy?

Mrs Stubbs: Y' cannot!

Terry: Y' can, Sammy said . . . .

Mrs Stubbs: I don't care what Sammy said. *You* can't go in water. What's the doctor said about swimmin' in your condition?

Terry: He hasn't mentioned it!

Mrs Stubbs: Not to you he hasn't, Terry, but he has to me.

Sammy: That's only up here though, mam. I've told y', when we're in Cornwall he won't know what asthma is. I'll take him swimmin' an' surf-boardin', we'll all do it, you'll do it, mam.

Mrs Stubbs: Go 'way! I couldn't do that. I'm far too old.

Sammy: Don't be soft. Y' not!

Mrs Stubbs: Surf-boardin' – these days if I went on the beach I'd have to wear a mac, not a bathin' suit.

Sammy: [*Emphatic*] Don't say that! You only say that while we're here. When we're in Cornwall you'll be as happy as the day's long an' y'll look like a queen.

Won't she, Terry?

Terry: Oh. Yeh. Yeh.

Sammy: Come on. Give work a miss tonight.

Mrs Stubbs: No, I better go, son. I've got to go out to the doctor's anyway so once I'm out I might as well go to work.

Sammy: The doctor's?

Mrs Stubbs: I need some more tablets so I might as well . . . .

Sammy: Tablets? Y' only got some last week. How many have you been takin'?

Mrs Stubbs: [*Getting her coat*] Not many. Now where's that . . . .

Sammy: Well, if y've not taken many, how come y' need some more?

Mrs Stubbs: I don't know, do I? They just go, Sammy. They just go.

Sammy: [*To* **Terry**] How many has she had today?

Terry: I dunno, do I?

Sammy: I told you to check. [*To his mother*] How many have y' had?

Mrs Stubbs: Sammy, stop goin' on, will y'? Look, I'm gonna be late for work.

Sammy: Look, I've told y', mam, y' shouldn't take them. They'll do y' no good. You don't need them, they're just drugs. They just make y' feel good for the minute but it's not a real feelin', mam, it's just a drug feelin'.

Mrs Stubbs: Drugs! Listen to him. Don't be stupid. They're tablets.

Sammy: But you shouldn't take them!

Mrs Stubbs: [*Rattled*] I know I *shouldn't*, son. But I do! I need them! Don't blame me, Sammy – before your father walked out this house, I'd never even taken an aspirin. When this was a proper family I didn't need to take tablets, so if you wanna start accusin' anyone, you accuse your father.

Sammy: Forget him. Why is it so different because he's not here? I do all right don't I? I look after y', don't I?

Mrs Stubbs: I know y' do, son. You're a good lad. And our Terry is. But we're not livin' in Cornwall, with the sea at the bottom of the garden. We're livin' here, now, an' I do need to take me tablets Sammy. So just lay off, will y'?

Sammy: [*To* **Terry**, *emphatic*] How many has she taken today?

Terry: [*His mother is looking at him*] What?

Sammy: Look, Terry. Tell me. I wanna know. [**Mrs Stubbs** *looks at* **Terry**, **Sammy** *looks at him.* **Terry** *is looking from one to the other*] Terry . . . y' not helpin' anyone. Y' might think y' are, but y' not. [**Terry** *remains silent*] Why are y' both deceivin' me?

Mrs Stubbs: [*Pause*] Don't take it out on Terry. I had four today.

Sammy: Jesus! Mam!

Mrs Stubbs: I'm sorry. I've got t' go to work. I'm gonna be late. [*She leaves*]

Terry: What did y' have to pick on her for?

Sammy: I wasn't pickin' on her.

Terry: You were.

Sammy: Look, Terry . . . .

Terry: Pickin' on her.

Sammy: Y' said y'd tell me how many she took. Why didn't y'?

Terry: I couldn't.

Sammy: Why not?

Terry: [*Pause, defiant*] I said I wouldn't tell y' cos she gave me some ciggies.

Sammy: You been smokin' again?

Terry: Yeh.

Sammy: [*Hitting him*] Get up to your room. Go on!

Terry: Get off, you!

Sammy: Go on. Get t' bed. Y' disgust me!

Terry: Get off!

Sammy: I'm warnin' y', Terry – get up there.

Terry: [*At the bottom of the stairs*] Get off me, you. You're not my old feller.

Sammy: Too right. An' it's a good job I'm not, isn't it? I might walk out like he did.

Terry: [*Running upstairs*] Sod off, you!

Sammy: [*Returns to the kitchen and sits at the table. Confused, he sighs. From upstairs we hear the sound of a forced wheezing cough.* **Sammy** *tries to ignore it. He tries to prepare his meal. But can't. He goes to the kitchen door and calls out*] Terry, shurrup, will y'? [*He goes back to preparing his meal but the wheezing plays on him. Eventually he gives in, bangs the pan down, and goes upstairs*]

21 Terry's bedroom

Terry *is on the bed, wheezing.* **Sammy** *opens the door.*

Sammy: Terry . . . stop it, will y'?

Terry: [*Near to tears*] It's you who brought this on!

Sammy: Stop it.

Terry: How would you like it if you had asthma?

Sammy: You know as well as I do that y' haven't got asthma.

Terry: Oh yeh. An' you know better than the bloody doctor, don't y'?

Sammy: Listen, Terry . . . he says it's asthma cos for the last four years me mam's been tellin' him you've got asthma. No matter what he said, she wouldn't believe him, cos she doesn't want to. In the end he just gave in an' agreed with her, to make her happy. He took the easy way out. Now you've started to believe it – when it suits y'. But it's not asthma. It's catarrh. It's just me mam wantin' y' t' stay like a kid forever, takin' the easy way out again, see. That's why I got narked about the pills, Terry; that's why I hit y'. It was because of the tablets – that's just another easy way out. But she shouldn't take them. Cos in the end, nothin's easy. The easy way's no way at all.

Terry: Go 'way!

Sammy: Look . . . I know I hit y' [*Going over to him*] I'm sorry, Terry. See, it's just like . . . like I'm trying t' get us organized – y' know what I mean? An' it just, it just gets me down if I'm tryin' t' get us t' Cornwall an' everyone's lettin' me down.

Terry: Goin' t' Cornwall! Don't be bloody stupid. How are we ever gonna get t' bloody Cornwall? It's just a lie. It's just a phoney – you just say that t' cheer me mam up.

Sammy: I don't, Terry. I mean it.

Terry: Yeh . . . well didn't anyone ever tell y' . . . y' need money t' get t' places like that, loads of money, an' how are you ever gonna get that?

Sammy: I've got money. Some. Already.

Terry: Oh yeh!

Sammy: [*Considers*] I'll show y'. Look. Come on. [*He goes out, calling as he does*] Here. [**Terry**, *curious, gets up from his bed*]

22   Sammy's bedroom

Sammy *is rolling back the carpet.* **Terry** *enters.*

Terry: What y' doin'?

Sammy: [*Prising up a floorboard*] Don't you ever tell anyone about this.

Terry: What is it?

Sammy: I know y' need money t' get t' Cornwall. What d' y' think this is? [*He pulls a cardboard box from beneath the floorboards, and opens it to reveal his savings*]

Terry: [*Impressed*] Where did y' get that?

Sammy: I earned it an' saved it. [*He takes out today's earnings and puts it with the rest of the money*] That's the beginnin' of the investment, our investment. That's ours. [*He replaces the box*]

23   The classroom

Mr Moore *is taking the register. He gets to the 'S's.*

Mr Moore: Stubbs . . . . [*He looks up, thinks and sees the class look at each other*]

First boy: What y' gonna do, sir?

Second boy: Y' can't do nott'n, can y', sir, if he doesn't wanna come in.

Third boy: 'Ey sir . . . send for Starsky an' Hutch, they'd bring Stubbsy in!

[*The class laughs,* **Mr Moore** *ignores it. He opens a drawer in his desk. The class falls silent, watching him. He produces a file, takes out an official absence sheet*]

First boy: He's takin' him to court.

Second boy: Stubbsy'll have to go to court.

Third boy: He's had it now, y' know.

First boy: [*To* **Mr Moore**] Will he, sir? Will Stubbsy have to go to court?

Mr Moore: [*Looking up from his writing*] Probably.

First boy: Ah 'ey, sir . . . couldn't y' give him a warnin' first?

Third boy: He's had loads of warnin's . . . hasn't he, sir? He's never in, is he?

First boy: Y' could give him another warnin', though, couldn't y', sir?

Mr Moore: [*Sighing*] What's the point? Sammy Stubbs has had warning after warning. He's ignored them all. I don't want to see him in court. But it's no longer up to me. Like it or loathe it, in this world there are rules, all sorts of rules. And if you break them, you pay the price. [*He resumes writing the official note, the class watches him, silenced*]

End of Part I

Part II

---

1   A city street

It is a brilliant spring morning in the city. **Sammy** *is walking through the crowds, dressed for summer.* **Rolo** *is running to catch up with* **Sammy**. *He is dressed as though winter is on the way, wearing a heavy coat.*

Rolo: Sammy! Sammy! [*He catches him up*] Why didn't you wait for me?

Sammy: I didn't know y' were gonna be saggin'. I thought y'd gone back t' school.

Rolo: I did, but it was crap. Anyway, who wants t' be in school on a day like this?

Sammy: Great, isn't it? I woke up dead early with the sun comin' in. I even heard the birds singin'. It's great.

Rolo: Yeh.

Sammy: Look at you though. What y' dressed like that for? Y'd think it was the middle of winter.

Rolo: Well I'd be no good wearin' gear like yours, would I?

Sammy: Why not? Let the air get t' y' body. Get a bit of sun an' blow the dust away.

Rolo: Yeh, an' where do I hide the gear?

Sammy: [*Pause*] Y' not goin' robbin' again, are y'?

Rolo: Why not?

Sammy: It wouldn't be so bad if y' robbed stuff that y' wanted. But y' just thieve stuff cos it's there.

Rolo: No I don't.

Sammy: What about that cheese grater the other day?

Rolo: Ah, that was just a practice. I'm goin' after real stuff today.

Sammy: Dressed like that?

Rolo: Yeh!

Sammy: [*Laughing*] Don't y' think y'll look a bit suspicious goin' round a shop like that when the sun's crackin' the flags?

Rolo: They take no notice of y', Sammy. I could've robbed the place soft the other day an' no one would've seen me. It's dead easy. There's nothin' to it.

Sammy: It'll catch up with y', Rolo. You do somethin' wrong an' it'll bring y' down in the end.

Rolo: Ah, sod off, you. You're just chicken.

2 Sammy's house

Terry *is watching the television test card. He is still in his pyjamas.* **Mrs Stubbs**, *a dress on, her hair tidied, comes in. She looks good. She switches the television off.*

Terry: Ah 'ey. I was watchin' that!

Mrs Stubbs: Well y' not watchin' it now. [*She goes to the window*] You get some clothes on. [*She opens the window*]

Terry: What y' doin' that for? It's freezin'.

Mrs Stubbs: Freezin'! It's a lovely day. Look . . . look at it . . . . [*She does a bit of a dance and sings the refrain from the song 'Lovely Day', followed by the line 'Oh What a Beautiful Morning'.* **Terry** *looks at her. Puzzled at first, but he smiles, and then laughs*]

Terry: Go 'way . . . you're a head case, mam!

Mrs Stubbs: [*Starts to approach him, mock threateningly. He leaps up from the chair, laughing, and moves to far side of room*] Right! [*Hand clap*] Come on. Upstairs and get some clothes on. We're not sittin' around lookin' at that thing today.

Terry: What's up?

Mrs Stubbs: I've decided, Terry.

Terry: What?

Mrs Stubbs: We're gonna decorate! I've decided. Come on. We'll get the walls stripped an' we'll go out an' get some new paper. We're gonna make the place look like it should look.

Terry: [*Amused by her sudden enthusiasm*] Why, mam?

Mrs Stubbs: Why son? I'll tell y' why – because it's a lovely day, because if I sit in that chair any longer I'll be an old woman this time next year, because I've decided we're gonna make a start. Here. [*Finds her bag*] Come on. [*Takes her tablets from the bag and goes upstairs*]

Terry: [*Following her up the stairs*] Ah 'ey, mam, y' know what Sammy said about the tablets. [*Pause*] He said they're no good for y'.

Mrs Stubbs: [*Opening the bathroom door*] Yeh, an' our Sammy's right! [*Opens the bottle, and empties* *the contents into the lavatory, and flushes it*] That's the end of them!

Terry: [*Alarmed*] What y' gonna do if y' need one?

Mrs Stubbs: I've decided I'm not goin' to need one. [*Points*] Right! Now you get dressed.

3 The warehouse

Sammy *and* **Rolo** *are talking.*

Rolo: Right. I'm off.

Sammy: Listen, Rolo . . . . Why don't y' stay here today?

Rolo: What for?

Sammy: What? Cos . . . cos I'm worried about y'.

Rolo: [*Laughing mockingly*] What d' y' wanna worry about me for?

Sammy: Because you need someone to worry about y'!

Rolo: [*Slightly embarrassed*] Get lost, you!

Sammy: What would your mum an' dad say, eh . . . if they knew you were thievin' from shops?

Rolo: They wouldn't say nothin', would they? Me ma goes robbin' sometimes. She tells me she's paid for the stuff but I know she hasn't. An' me old feller wouldn't care. He doesn't care about anythin'.

Sammy: I'll bet he does, Rolo. I'll bet he cares about you.

Rolo: How d'you know, eh?

Sammy: I just do. If he knew y' were robbin' shops I'll bet y' he'd be really upset.

Rolo: Go 'way, you. Y' mental!

Sammy: Your old feller should be keepin' an eye on you. If I was your dad I'd knock seven kinds of sunshine out of you – that'd stop y'! [**Rolo** *is incredulous*] I'd sort you out if I was your old feller.

Rolo: Well y' not my old feller, are y' . . . so shut it. [*Pause.* **Rolo** *is upset*] Bleedin' goin' on to me. What's it got to do with you, eh?

Sammy: I'm just tellin' y', aren't I?

Rolo: Yeh. Well, don't! [*He is offended but is unsure why*] You goin' on about my old feller – what about your own? Walked out years ago, didn't he? Don't go on about my dad. He didn't walk out on us.

Sammy: He might just as well have done though, mightn't he, eh? The amount you care about him. An' he doesn't look after you too well, does he?

Rolo: Sod off, you. I'm goin'. I'm not listenin' to this! [*Going*]

Sammy: Stay here, Rolo . . . .

Rolo: With you? Huh . . . I'd rather be in a swimmin' pool with Jaws. [*He goes.* **Sammy** *watches him until his thoughts are interrupted by a car horn.* **Mr Derbyshire** *has driven up and is waiting to park*]

Mr Derbyshire: Morning, Sammy . . . any spaces over there?

Sammy: Oh hello, Mr D. Just hold on . . . I'll have a look for y' . . . .

4 Sammy's house

Mrs Stubbs *and* **Terry** *are moving a sideboard across the room.*

Terry: Ah 'ey, mam . . . can't we have the telly on while we're doin' this?

Mrs Stubbs: No!

Terry: Ah . . . .

Mrs Stubbs: Let's have the radio on. We haven't had music in this house for years . . . where is it? [*She pulls a battered transistor radio out of a cupboard and switches on. There is a faulty buzz*]

Terry: It's bust.

Mrs Stubbs: Oh well . . . .

Terry: What we should have is a music centre. I'd love one of them.

Mrs Stubbs: I'd like one meself, son. Music all day long, records as well as the radio.

Terry: An' tapes, mam . . . they have cassette players in them now. [*She stares at him. He becomes slightly uncomfortable under her gaze*] What y' lookin' at, mam?

Mrs Stubbs: [*Smiling*] You're gettin' to that age now, aren't y'? Starting to take an interest in music. It'll be the girls next, won't it?

Terry: [*Embarrassed*] Go 'way.

Mrs Stubbs: [*Laughing*] Ah . . . you will. [**Terry** *is still embarrassed.* **Mrs Stubbs** *is now moving the next piece of furniture.* **Terry** *grabs the other end*] When I first started listenin' to music it was the Liverpool groups that were all the rage. I had a little transistor that me mam bought me. I used to listen to it under the bedclothes at night.

Terry: [*Smiling, warm*] Did y'?

Mrs Stubbs: I used to go an' watch all the groups – they had clubs in those days that were open at dinner time an' y' could get in for one and six. We used to go dancin' an' watchin' the groups, me an' the girls. We should have been at school, but we didn't care. [*A knock on the door*] I'll move this, Terry. You see who it is. [**Terry** *exits. She puts down the piece of furniture and looks at the wall, planning her wallpaper*] Yellow . . . a nice bright yellow.

Terry: [*Enters with a recorded delivery letter and book to sign for it*] It's the postie, mam. Y've got t' sign for it.

Mrs Stubbs: What is it? [*She signs and* **Terry** *exits with the pen and book. She begins to open the envelope*] Well, we might have come up on the pools but that's not very likely, seein' as we don't do the pools.

Terry: [*Re-entering*] Go on, mam . . . tell us about the music an' the clubs an' that . . . go on. I like it when y' talk about the olden days . . . go on, y' know, about when y' were a girl an' that . . . .

Mrs Stubbs: Oh, Christ! It's a summons. They're takin' me t' court.

5   The department store

Rolo *is standing near a display of lighters, in a glass cabinet. A closed-circuit camera is panning over the goods.* **Rolo** *watches until the camera is off him, then stretches a hand round the glass cabinet. He takes an expensive-looking lighter.*

6   The warehouse

Mr Derbyshire *enters.*

Mr Derbyshire: How's it going then, Sammy? How's business been?

Sammy: OK, Mr D.

Mr Derbyshire: Glad to hear it. Always glad to hear of a business colleague doing well.

Sammy: I've been thinking about this café, Mr D.

Mr Derbyshire: About what?

Sammy: The café, y' know, the restaurant, here in this place . . . .

Mr Derbyshire: Oh, yes, yes, yes . . . I know. I like to meet a young lad with initiative . . . very good.

Sammy: Well look, Mr D. Have y' given it some thought?

Mr Derbyshire: A lot . . . oh, yes.

Sammy: Cos, listen, I've had this great idea: y' know, like, in most cafés, y' know if y' go in with kids, little kids, well, what happens? They're not interested in sittin' at tables, are they? They start cryin', don't they, an' makin' a noise an' upsettin' other customers an' no one gets any peace, do they? So look . . . what we do is we partition off a bit of the restaurant, like say this area, over here . . . an' we put toys in there so that kids can play while the grown ups are eatin', see what I mean? A play space for the kids – simple, isn't it?

Mr Derbyshire: Well. You've, em . . . certainly been er . . . thinking . . . haven't you?

Sammy: That's all it takes, Mr D. A bit of thought. Mind you . . . that's only the start, I mean . . . .

Mr Derbyshire: I'm sure, you . . . but I must get on, Sammy. We, em, business people, we must keep on. Full day for me today.

Sammy: OK, Mr D. See y' later, eh? You give that some thought, eh?

Mr Derbyshire: Yes. I certainly will. Cheerio now.

Sammy: Tarar, Mr D.

7 Sammy's house

Mrs Stubbs *is sitting in her chair.*

Mrs Stubbs: Where's me tablets?

Terry: Down the bog. Y' don't need them, mam.

Mrs Stubbs: Don't I? An' who's gonna pay for this, eh? Where am I gonna find the money to pay a fine? [*She sighs*] There's no point. No point. Y' try an' get on y' feet . . . an' what happens?

Terry: It's not your worry, mam. It's Sammy's. Let him pay it.

Mrs Stubbs: Hmm!

Terry: Don't worry, mam. Mam, don't worry. [*Pause*] Sammy's got a hundred quid upstairs.

Mrs Stubbs: Are you tryin' to be funny?

Terry: No, honest. He's saved it up.

Mrs Stubbs: Y' jokin'.

Terry: I'm not. Come on . . . I'll show y'. [*He gets up*]

8 The department store

A display of clocks. **Rolo** *stretches out his hand. A man is watching him.*

9 Sammy's house

Terry *and* **Mrs Stubbs** *are in the lounge, with* **Sammy's** *box of money.*

Terry: I told y'.

Mrs Stubbs: Where did this come from?

Terry: He saved it. Y' know all the jobs. It's for goin' t' Cornwall.

Mrs Stubbs: God, Cornwall!

Terry: But he'll have t' pay the fine with it, mam.

Mrs Stubbs: [*Pause*] He's a dreamer. [*Pause*] Cornwall . . . us goin' t' live in Cornwall! [*Pause*] I felt so good this mornin' an' all. I didn't want to mope around. But as soon as y' start lookin' up, y' get knocked back again. [*She picks up the money*] What I could do with this!

Terry: That'll cover the fine, mam.

Mrs Stubbs: [*Looking at the money*] Yeh. Mind you, it takes ages for a court case to come up, doesn't it?

Terry: What?

Mrs Stubbs: We're never gonna get to Cornwall, are we?

Terry: I dunno, mam.

Mrs Stubbs: [*Looking at the money*] Sod it! [*Moving out*] Come on.

Terry: Where?

Mrs Stubbs: I wanted to feel good today. Well, I'm goin' to.

Terry: But y've got no tablets, mam.

Mrs Stubbs: I know, but I've got this, [*Indicating the money*] haven't I?

Terry: That's our Sammy's.

Mrs Stubbs: Why did he save it? He saved it for us, didn't he? So we could go away. Well I don't wanna go away. I wanna make this place look like it should, bring a bit of life into the place. Our Sammy'll understand. Come on. [*She gets her coat*]

10   The car park

Sammy *is sitting on the car park wall, counting out his earnings, putting coins into piles. When a car horn sounds,* **Sammy** *looks up and quickly returns the money to his pocket. He waves the car down and runs across to a parking space, waving the driver in.*

11   The department store

A store detective is watching **Rolo**.

12   The car park

Sammy *throws a coin in the air, catches it and puts it in his pocket. He pulls out a cloth and begins polishing the car he has just waved in. He is in high spirits.*

13   The department store

Rolo *is heading for the main door, but the store detective is standing at the door. When* **Rolo** *gets to the door, the detective blocks his way.*

Detective: [*Taking his arm. Quietly but firmly*] Right, son, come with me.

Rolo: Get off! I haven't done nothin'. Why y' pickin' on me? I haven't touched nott'n, honest. I wouldn't. [*An alarm clock falls out from under his coat*] It's, er m . . . me watch's bust. Me mam lent me the clock. T' tell the time. [*Two plant pots fall out from his coat. The* **Detective** *looks at the pots, and then at* **Rolo**]

Detective: An' what in the name of God do you want with plant pots?

Rolo: [*Sheepish*] I dunno.

Detective: [*Sighing*] That's the worst thing about

this job, son – most of the people I catch have taken stuff that's worthless to them. [*He calls out to the commissionaire*] Wally. Here. [*To* **Rolo**] Why do you risk it for somethin' y' don't need?

Rolo: I dunno.

Detective: Wally . . . take this lad to Mr Benedict's office, will y'?

Wally: Yes, sir. [**Wally** *takes* **Rolo** *by the arm. The commissionaire is* **Mr Derbyshire**]

14 Sammy's house

Sammy *comes in through the front door. There are rolls of wallpaper on the floor, and music is coming from the lounge. In the lounge,* **Mrs Stubbs** *and* **Terry** *are stripping wallpaper. The music comes from a new music centre.* **Sammy***, excited, comes into the lounge.*

Sammy: [*As he enters*] Mam . . . look how much I made today! [*He registers what is happening*] What's this?

Mrs Stubbs: Decoration time, son.

Sammy: What's that? [*Indicating the music centre*]

Terry: It's a stereogram, Sammy. It's got a cassette player an' a record deck an' a . . . .

Sammy: Where did it come from?

Mrs Stubbs: Look, Sammy, [*Going across to him*] I know y' were savin' that money for us, I know y' wanted to make me happy . . . but . . . well this makes me happy, son.

Terry: Sammy . . . me mam hasn't taken a tablet all day.

Sammy: You've spent it!

Mrs Stubbs: Eh . . . we've got something for you as well, y' know. [*Grabbing a box: it is a plug-in television soccer game*] Here.

Sammy: It's trash . . . all of it's trash. You've spent my money on trash. It was for Cornwall.

Mrs Stubbs: [*Showing her authority*] Oh, come off it, Sammy. How the hell we ever gonna get to Cornwall? Y' livin' in your head, Sammy. Now isn't it better to do somethin' sensible with the money? At least this way we all get a lift from it. And we need one! Look, [*Showing him the summons*] we're bein' prosecuted, Sammy. I've got to go to court because you've been saggin' school.

Sammy: But I saved that money, I worked for it an' saved it. An' you've just blown it on a pile of trash. What have y' done?

Mrs Stubbs: [*Slightly riled*] Well at least I've made him happy . . . an' me.

Sammy: [*Shouting*] For how long? What y' gonna do when y' bored with it, eh?

Mrs Stubbs: Now come on, Sammy, the . . . .

Sammy: How am I gonna take y' anywhere, do anythin' for y' if this is the way y' carry on?

Mrs Stubbs: Sammy, there's no need for this.

Sammy: Isn't there?

Mrs Stubbs: [*Shouting*] If you'd gone to school when y' should've done . . . .

Sammy: School – what I did – the money I earned – that was more important than going to school.

Mrs Stubbs: [*Stunned*] You what? [**Sammy** *turns and storms out*]

15 The car park: early next day

Only a few cars are parked. **Mr Derbyshire's** *car is pulling in.*

16 The warehouse

Sammy *is asleep.*

17 The car park

Mr Derbyshire *has parked, is getting out of his car and looking for change. He cannot find any, and looks across to the warehouse.*

18 The warehouse

Sammy *is waking up, stretching, and getting up.*

Mr Derbyshire: [*Entering*] Sammy! [**Sammy** *is slightly startled*] You've saved my bacon. Could you let me have some change for the meter? I don't know what my mind's coming to lately.

Sammy: [*Searching his pockets for change*] How much?

Mr Derbyshire: I've only got a fifty . . . can you change that? Oh, hold on. [*Puts his car keys down and looks in his pockets*] Oh . . . . [*Gives* **Sammy** *the fifty*] Let me have that. Keep the change. Right. Must get off. It's all go in my business, Sammy. An early meeting.

Sammy: [*Almost blocking his exit*] Listen, Mr D, have y' made up y' mind?

Mr Derbyshire: What about? Look I'm in an awful rush.

Sammy: What about? About the café . . . about this place?

Mr Derbyshire: Look, Sammy. I mean . . . .

Sammy: You're gonna do it, aren't y'? Y' gonna build a café here . . . like y' said, aren't y'? Like you said, with me runnin' it.

Mr Derbyshire: I never said that. You did.

Sammy: [*Looking at him. Pause*] An' aren't y' gonna do it?

Mr Derbyshire: Now look. As far as I know, and it's not my department really, as far as I know, this place is coming down. It'll probably be replaced by an extension for the car park, a multi-storey . . . .

Sammy: A car park! An' what good's a car park gonna be?

Mr Derbyshire: You . . . you might be able to get a job in it. They'll need people in the booths and if I put a word . . . .

Sammy: No . . . no. You can't do it.

Mr Derbyshire: [*A little anxious*] Well it's not me that's doing it. It's my . . . my company.

Sammy: Well, tell them. It's your company . . . you tell them!

Mr Derbyshire: Well . . . it's not, it's not *my* company in that sense.

Sammy: What?

Mr Derbyshire: Look . . . I'm going to be very late. I've got to . . . .

Sammy: [*Blocking his entrance*] Tell me what y' mean! Tell me!

Mr Derbyshire: Well . . . I mean, you didn't think . . . I mean . . . people say that, don't they, 'my company', 'my firm', but that doesn't mean it's their company in that sense.

Sammy: You don't own your company?

Mr Derbyshire: When I say 'my company', Sammy, what I mean is the company I work for.

[*Pause.* **Sammy** *is stunned*]

Sammy: You liar! [**Mr Derbyshire** *is frightened*] You lied! [**Sammy** *walking towards him*] You wanted me to think it was your company. That you owned it.

Mr Derbyshire: Sammy, the . . . .

Sammy: Don't. Don't you give me any more lies.

Mr Derbyshire: I'm sorry. I didn't mean to deceive you. [*He is frightened*] I'm sorry . . . it's just something I've said for years, 'my company'. It's not a lie. If people think I'm a director then it's up to them – but it's not a lie. It's just something I say. It doesn't hurt anybody. [**Sammy** *stares at him, blocking his exit still*] I'm going to be late.

Sammy: [*Quietly*] Get out.

[**Mr Derbyshire** *rapidly makes his exit.* **Sammy** *sees the keys and picks them up. Goes to door with them. Just as he is about to shout* **Rolo** *enters*]

Rolo: Were you talkin' to him?

Sammy: What? Yeh.

Rolo: Why?

Sammy: He's the feller who was gonna build the restaurant, I was tellin' y' about.

Rolo: Get lost. Him? He's a doorman in one of the stores.

Sammy: What? No, he's not.

Rolo: He is. He took me in yesterday. I got caught. They're prosecutin' me.

Sammy: An' me. For not goin' t' school.

Rolo: [*Laughing*] Head case. Why didn't y' go back when they warned y'?

Sammy: I dunno. I just pretended it didn't matter.

Rolo: I told y' y' were a loony. Is that what he told y', that feller? That he was gonna build a café? [*Laughing*] An' you believed him. [*Laughing*]

Sammy: [*Looks at* **Rolo**, *and then at the keys in his hand*] 'Ey, Rolo. D' y' fancy comin' t' Cornwall? [**Rolo** *stops laughing and looks at* **Sammy**]

19   A motorway service area

Mr Derbyshire's *car is being driven along the south-bound carriageway of the motorway, towards the service area.* **Rolo** *and* **Sammy** *are in the car.*

Rolo: Pull into that place. We'll get some stuff there.

Sammy: We've got no money.

Rolo: We've got fingers though. Come on, pull over.

Sammy: I don't think I know how to stop it.

Rolo: Don't be soft. Y' just slow down an' then press the brake. [*The car pulls into the service area car park. It stops.* **Rolo** *gets out*] Come on. Y' all right? There's no coppers around.

20 The service area shop

Rolo *and* **Sammy** *enter. It is a small self service shop, with a cash desk at the exit.* **Rolo** *lifts a bar of chocolate, mazagines, souvenirs. He keeps looking at* **Sammy** *and motioning him to do the same.* **Sammy** *can't.*

Rolo: [*Whispering*] What's up? Come on . . . . There's nothin' to it. [*He picks up a map*] Here. [*He forces it on* **Sammy** *who checks that no one is looking and then hides it*] That's it. [**Rolo** *continues his robbing, with* **Sammy** *watching him. Finally,* **Sammy** *replaces the map and leaves. He goes out to the car.* **Rolo** *comes after him*]

Rolo: Oh . . . you were great, weren't y'? Streuth we're gonna live well in Cornwall with you carryin' on like that, aren't we? [*He offers* **Sammy** *a bar of chocolate*] Here! [**Sammy** *doesn't take it*]

Sammy: I'm not hungry.

Rolo: [*Taking it back*] I'm starvin'. They're great, these. Go on . . . tell us about Cornwall again, all about the surfin' an' that . . . go on, it's great that.

Sammy: There's er . . . [*Goes into thought*]

Rolo: Well, go on.

Sammy: There's, er, coves . . . an', er, sandy beaches . . . .

Rolo: An' we're gonna live there. Swimmin' every day . . . oh what . . . I can't wait. Go on, tell us about all the smugglers there in the old days. I'd love t' be a smuggler. Go on . . . tell us about that.

Sammy: Nah.

Rolo: Ah, go on. I love hearin' all about that. You're good at tellin' it.

Sammy: Yeh. I'm very good at stories, Rolo. [*They get in the car*]

21   In the car on the motorway

Sammy: 'Ey, Rolo . . . .

Rolo: What?

Sammy: I'm sorry.

Rolo: What about?

Sammy: It's just another lie, Rolo. We'd never get t' Cornwall.

Rolo: Y' what?

Sammy: It's stupid. [*The car pulls off on to a slip road*]

Rolo: Where y' goin'? Where y' goin'? This isn't the way t' Cornwall!

Sammy: I know. This isn't the way to anywhere. [*The car turns right and makes its way along a road over the motorway*] We're goin' home, Rolo.

Rolo: Sammy . . . we're not! We're goin' t' Cornwall.

Sammy: No, we're not. [*The car turns right on to an approach slip road, back on to the northbound carriageway of the motorway*]

Rolo: [*Apoplectic*] Y' stupid . . . what y' . . . stupid . . . . Look . . . . You bleedin' loony, head case . . . y' . . . y' . . . Sammy! Sammy! Turn round . . . turn round . . . .

Sammy: [*Throughout* **Rolo's** *dialogue*] We're goin' home, an' you're goin' t' court, an' I'm goin' t' court, an' that's real that is . . . .

The end

Uncle Sangi
Tom Hadaway

First broadcast by B B C School Television for the series
Scene

Characters

Uncle Sangi
Mr Dev, Sangi's brother
Mrs Dev
Sharm, their son
Mr Thompson, an old age pensioner
Neighbour
Police officer
Taxi driver

Non-speaking parts:

another policeman
man on a park bench
teenagers in the park

Mr Dev (played by Madhav Sharma) in the B B C pro-
duction of Uncle Sangi

Uncle Sangi

---

1 Outside North Shields railway station

Passengers are leaving the station after a train has arrived. Last out, and in a careful manner is Uncle Sangi. He moves towards the taxi rank, but noticing a police officer turns instead to study the magazines on the kiosk.

  His actions are furtive. He glances sideways to see if the officer has moved on, then he makes his way to a taxi. He consults the driver, indicating an address on a slip of paper. He climbs into the taxi and it moves off.

2 An Asian general dealer's shop

A brief view, establishing the exterior of the shop.

3 The interior of the shop

Mr Dev *is serving an old age pensioner.* **Mrs Dev** *is replenishing the shelves with stock.*

OAP: [*Aggrieved*] Seventy-five pence?

Mr Dev: [*Apologetic*] I know, I know.

OAP: It's not right, man! Every week, up and up.

Mr Dev: Believe me, Mr Thompson, the supermarket is charging ninety for the same tin.

OAP: I can't find things in supermarkets.

Mr Dev: No, and they will not sell you two eggs, eh? You want two eggs, I will sell you two eggs.

OAP: I'll hev ti think about where I take me custom.

Mr Dev: Mr Thompson, you are one of my first customers. If I was not a fair man you would not come here every week for five years.

OAP: Seventy-five pence!

Mr Dev: World shortage of protein, Mr Thompson. You know what that means.

OAP: No, I don't.

Mr Dev: Not enough of what everybody is wanting. A price has to be paid. [**Sharm** *enters with his dog coming from the rear premises*] Sharm! Where you going?

Sharm: Taking the dog out, da.

Mr Dev: Then you are not taking him out through here.

Sharm: Oh, da!

Mr Dev: And I am not your dad! I am your father.

Mrs Dev: Don't let us be hearing all that again, please.

Mr Dev: No, no. I don't like this word da. To my father I was not allowed to speak . . . .

Mrs Dev: Please!

Sharm: Just taking the dog.

Mr Dev: Look! I should not have to explain. [*To the* **OAP**] Excuse me! [*He goes to the window, and turns round a notice. It reads: 'No dogs allowed in the interest of hygiene*]' What does that say? No dogs allowed! You understand. I say to my customers, 'No dogs'. It is a rule, and who makes the rules, it has to be the same for everyone. No exceptions. That is fairness.

Sharm: Aw, but . . . .

Mrs Dev: Do as your father tells you.

Mr Dev: No dogs! [*He returns to the customer. The shop door opens.* **Uncle Sangi** *enters. He smiles expectantly, hoping to be welcome.* **Mr Dev** *stiffens. He has not seen his brother for several years. He is uneasy at this unexpected arrival.* **Mrs Dev** *registers a faint smile, which changes quickly to apprehension as she glances toward her husband*]

OAP: I'll just take it.

Mr Dev: Pardon?

OAP: Seventy-five pence. [*He hands over the correct money*] I'll jus' take it.

Mr Dev: [*Finishes serving the* **OAP**, *escorts him to the door, closing it after him, securing the catch. The two brothers pause to regard each other, then suddenly embrace*] Sangi!

Sangi: Manjit! [**Uncle Sangi** *glances anxiously behind, through the window.* **Mr Dev** *follows the glance*]

Mr Dev: [*In Punjabi*] Come! [*He ushers his brother through to the rear premises.* **Uncle Sangi** *pauses to salute* **Mrs Dev**. *They exit.* **Sharm** *looks on, bewildered by this sudden adult display*]

Sharm: Who's that, ma?

Mrs Dev: Your Uncle Sangi.

Sharm: The black sheep?

Mrs Dev: Ssssh!

Sharm: But you said . . . .

Mrs Dev: Don't be silly.

Sharm: Where's he come from?

Mrs Dev: Take the dog.

Sharm: Somethin' up, ma?

Mrs Dev: Questions!

Sharm: But, ma . . . .

Mrs Dev: Go on, take the dog . . . . Maybe you find out when you come back.

4   A narrow lane behind the shop

Sharm *comes through the yard door, the dog at his heels.* **Mr Dev's** *bin is outside the door. A neighbour intercepts* **Sharm**.

Neighbour: Hey! You!

Sharm: What?

Neighbour: Tell your father ti shift that bin.

Sharm: What for?

Neighbour: Cos it's got the lane blocked, that's what for. Tell'm ti shift it.

Sharm: Tell him yourself.

Neighbour: Don't cheek me.

Sharm: Not cheeking you.

Neighbour: Place is like a tip. Wasn't like this when Jackson had the shop.

Sharm: Who was Jackson?

Neighbour: A bloody white man.

Sharm: Oh, is that a fact? [*Moves off. Retorts*] What made him bloody? You punch his nose or something?

Neighbour: You . . . damn Paki.

5   Mr Dev's house at the back of the shop: the passageway outside the living room

Mrs Dev *is struggling through the doorway into the living room with a tray of tea things. Her husband and* **Uncle Sangi** *are heard talking in Pubjabi.* **Mrs Dev** *passes through into the living room and closes the door behind her.*

Mr Dev: Trouble! You talk to me of trouble!

Sangi: Everywhere there is trouble.

   [**Mrs Dev** *passes through into the living room and closes the door behind her*]

6   The living room

There is a coffee table, settee, and easy chairs. Some of the shop's grocery stores are stocked in the room. An old Victorian print of highland cattle hangs alongside a picture of the Guru Nanak (the founder of Sikhism).
   Mr Dev *and* **Uncle Sangi** *are seated.* **Mrs Dev** *is serving them with tea. She places the cups, milk, sugar, a plate of biscuits and a bowl of nuts beside the men. Her manner of serving is studied, meticulous, and formal.*

Mr Dev: [*Continuing in English*] Trouble! You talk to me of trouble.

Sangi: Everywhere there is trouble.

Mrs Dev: [*Setting down the tray*] Everywhere!

Mr Dev: No, no. Trouble is not finding trouble. Trouble is making trouble. [*Pause*]

Mrs Dev: I am from Jullunder, but making head or tail of that is beyond me. [**Sangi** *grins*]

Mr Dev: Don't be frivolous.

Mrs Dev: [*To* **Sangi**] You remember Jacinda? She was Jullunder girl. Went to Birmingham, let me see, must be five, six years now.

Sangi: Birmingham is a very big place.

Mrs Dev: Jacinda was a very big girl.

Sangi: Not as big as Birmingham.

Mrs Dev: But very nearly . . . you remember? [*They laugh. But* **Mr Dev** *does not join in*]

Mr Dev: Listen! I am talking seriously, and someone else is making trouble, I am taking no notice.

Sangi: Manjit! I am your brother.

Mrs Dev: [*Endorsing, in Punjabi*] Your brother.

Mr Dev: You should have had the papers, Sangi.

Sangi: Do I need papers to say I am your brother?

Mrs Dev: Your brother.

Mr Dev: Woman! You are sounding like a budgie.

Mrs Dev: It is my opinion . . . .

Mr Dev: [*In Punjabi*] Shut up! [*Embarrassed pause*]

Mrs Dev: Have your tea, Sangi.

Sangi: Thank you.

Mr Dev: I am saying, the Home Office . . . .

Sangi: I tell you it was a trick. 'We will catch the half of them.' This is how they are thinking. Amnesty! For every hundred coming out, only fifty are being approved. Immigration are settling for that.

Mr Dev: No. No.

Sangi: Manjit! I am only asking, give me a month . . . three weeks! Look, it is their rule, they must apply for a warrant, by the time it comes, whoosh! I am away.

Mr Dev: No, no. No warrant business now. It's slap,

bang, got you. It's all right for you, Sangi, you get caught, you are shipped out. I have a business, a family. They charge me help you evade Immigration, I am for the bloody high jump.

Sangi: Business and family. Jullunder, Newcastle upon Tyne, every inch, shopkeeper.

Mr Dev: That is not fair, and what have you been doing all these years?

Sangi: You want all the nasty details?

Mr Dev: What bad people are you mixing with?

Sangi: And you think we can choose our company?

7 A park

There is a notice: 'Dogs must be kept on leads at all times.'

Sharm *is with his dog. He watches a group of four or five white youths, teenagers, playing football. They have put their coats down for improvised goalposts.* **Sharm** *would like to join in, but he is not invited. The ball comes across to him. He dutifully retrieves it. The youths carry on ignoring his presence.*

Sharm *leaves, walking across the grass. He takes a small tennis ball from his pocket and dribbles it. The dog attempts to pick it up. A man on a park bench lowers his newspaper and glances severely over.* **Sharm**, *aware of the man watching, feels foolish and picks up the ball. He moves on.*

Two white teenage girls pass. He sideglances at them. They stare boldly back at him, put their heads together, smiling, obviously making him the subject of comment. He hurriedly drops his gaze.

Everywhere in the park people are together. **Sharm** *is alone except for his dog.*

8   The kitchen, at home

It is now a week later. **Mrs Dev** *is clearing up breakfast.*
Sharm *comes in from the yard.*

Sharm: Where's da?

Mrs Dev: Cash and carry. You should be helping.

Sharm: Supposed to be on holiday.

Mrs Dev: Your father gets no holiday.

Sharm: Stuck with a stupid shop, that's why.

Mrs Dev: Don't talk silly.

Sharm: Should get a decent job.

Mrs Dev: What do you know about getting jobs?
Here! You want job. Take this to Uncle Sangi. [*She
hands him a breakfast tray*]

Sharm: What's he do for a job?

Mrs Dev: Lot of things. A farmer, a sailor, oh! lot of
things.

Sharm: But what's he do now?

Mrs Dev: He's Jack of all trades. Here! [*She puts the
sugar on the tray*]

Sharm: Why's he never go out, ma?

Mrs Dev: What you mean?

Sharm: Hardly ever goes out. Jus' sits upstairs.

Mrs Dev: That's his business. Go on.

Sharm: Maybe he's a secret agent.

Mrs Dev: Hmmm!

Sharm: Maybe he works for the C I A.

Mrs Dev: Maybe you are a silly lump.

Sharm: Well, he could be for all I know.

Mrs Dev: Go on with you.

9 Uncle Sangi's bedroom

Uncle Sangi *is sitting at a small table beside the window. He is cleaning a pistol. There is a knock at the door. Hurriedly* **Uncle Sangi** *puts his gun into his suitcase.*

Sangi: [*In Punjabi*] Come in. [**Sharm** *enters with the breakfast tray*] Good morning, Sharm. That looks good. And what's my brother's son up to today?

Sharm: [*Not comprehending*] Sorry!

Sangi: OK.

Sharm: I've nearly forgotten our language.

Sangi: Oh!

Sharm: English all day at school, you know.

Sangi: That's all right.

Sharm: Times I cannot follow my ma an' da. If they yak on too fast.

Sangi: Huh!

Sharm: They yak on fast sometimes, so's I won't.

Sangi: What they tell you about me? [**Sharm** *shakes his head signifying very little*] Why I come here?

Sharm: No.

Sangi: Hmmm! You keep a secret, Sharm? [**Sharm** *nods his head in agreement*] I am a special agent. Very hush-hush, OK?

Sharm: OK.

Sangi: Hey! Where you take your dog today?

Sharm: Down along the docks. By the woodyard. There's rabbits there, he sniffs them out.

Sangi: You mind if I come?

Sharm: Why, aye! man.

Sangi: Good!

10   A dock road, on the north bank of the Tyne

There are derelict coal staiths, timber yards, and areas of wasteland. The roadways are deserted. **Uncle Sangi**, **Sharm**, *and the dog walk along a track, and then they settle down on a grass slope, and look across at the ships.*

Sangi: [*Relaxing*] Hey! It's good here. Good to see ships again. You see ships, you remember all those places in the world you can go . . . anytime. Trincomalee! Port Said! Durban, Melbourne! . . . 'Frisco!

Sharm: You been all those places?

Sangi: How you say, 'Why, aye, man'? Some maybe two, three times.

Sharm: Must be great that. It's what I really fancy myself. Travelling.

Sangi: All us Punjabi are travellers. Huh! I think maybe God ran out of human souls, and gave us the souls of birds. Maybe he wasn't expecting so many people.

Sharm: Better than being stuck in a shop.

Sangi: But you got to belong somewhere, Sharm. You just got to belong somewhere. Cos everywhere you go,

someone sure say, 'An' where you come from then?'
Straightway you got to say exactly where you belong.
[*The dog nuzzles into* **Sangi**] Hey, fella. Where you
belong, eh? You belong Newcastle upon Tyne. 'Why,
aye, man!'

Sharm: You like dogs, Uncle Sangi?

Sangi: Sure! They OK. I had a dog. 'Board ship! Little
black fella like me. Hmm! Never went ashore. Everybody's pal, but like special to me. Maybe cos all the
time I feed it, it thinks I'm God, y'know? Got this
trouble in its ear, all yella stuff comin' out, y' know?
Skipper say, 'Sangi! your dog too sick, you gotta put
him down.' I couldn't do it, man! So skipper say,
'Leave it to me.' But that dog, hey! He growl, deep
down. I think he knew he go overboard in a canvas
bag with some chain, or maybe his throat gets cut,
y'know? Well, you gotta be honest with a dog. Man!
they read your mind, like people can't do. Life an'
death. God got to do his own dirty work. So I took him
to his favourite place, up on the fo'csle point, and
Bang! I shoot him through the head with me gun. All
the time, he jus' stand quiet, an' calm like, y'know?
Like he knew I was being fair with him. [*Pause*]

Sharm: Me da says, they're just dirty, messy things.

Sangi: Maybe! But we say the cow is a holy animal,
an' they's dirty, messy things, eh? Only bigger.

Sharm: You still believe all that religion stuff?

Sangi: Oh! In Birmingham cows is extinct.

Sharm: I mean, Guru Nanak, and all that?

Sangi: Huh! Long time since Sangi inside the
Gurdwara!

Sharm: Ma makes me go. Just once a month like.

Sangi: You wear your turban?

Sharm: No chance! Kids all just scoff. Get called Dick Turban.

Sangi: Who's he?

Sharm: Some Englishman. Rode around on a horse, robbing and pinching.

Sangi: You don't like that, eh? Being called Dick Turban?

Sharm: No. Not any more.

Sangi: Come on, we walk on. [*They get up and move along the river bank. The dog runs ahead*]

Sangi: I tell you somethin' else about dogs. There's good, there's bad. But you don't ever get a dog tell you lies. Dogs! They never learn talk. So they don't tell you no lies, an' they don't call you no names. [*Pause*] Sure, I like dogs, Sharm. [*Placing his arm comfortably around the boy's shoulder, they walk on*]

11 The shop

Sharm *is sweeping and tidying up. He wears a white apron. The shop door is open. Outside there is the sound of a car engine.* **Mrs Dev** *comes through from the rear of the premises. She is unusually glamorous, with make-up, earrings and a new sari. Searching through her handbag, she makes sure she has everything. The car horn sounds an impatient note.*

Mr Dev: [*From outside in Punjabi*] You hurrying yourself up?

Mrs Dev: [*In Punjabi*] Coming! Coming!

Sharm: Who's on tonight, ma? Shashi Kapoor?

Mrs Dev: Oh, no. [*Ecstatically*] Amitab Bachan!

Sharm: Ooo! Amitab Bachan! Got plenty paper hankies, then?

Mrs Dev: Ooh! he's lovely. [*There is another urgent toot of the horn*] All right! All right! [*She remembers to go to the sweet counter, and helps herself to a favourite packet of sweets*]

Mrs Dev: Now, be a good boy.

Sharm: Aye, ma!

Mrs Dev: Finish tidy up. Lock the door properly. And, not too late to bed.

Sharm: Aye, ma.

Mrs Dev: [*Embraces* **Sharm**, *and gives him a kiss. Calling in Punjabi*] Coming! Coming! [*To* **Sharm** *in Punjabi*] Goodbye!

Sharm: [*In Punjabi*] Goodbye! [*In English*] Enjoy it. [**Mrs Dev** *exits, the car revs up outside*]

Mrs Dev: [*Calling to* **Sharm**] Uncle Sangi was fancying some pickle onions!

The car drives off. **Sharm** *closes the door and fastens the catch. He goes to the shelves. Collects a jar of onions, some packets of crisps and a bottle of cider. He picks up his box of sweepings, and goes into the passageway. He calls up to* **Uncle Sangi**]

Sharm: They're off. Amitab Bachan! Three and a half hours solid blubbing and crying. Jesmond Picture House be like a swimming pool.

12 The backyard behind the shop

Sharm *comes out with a cardboard box. The dog jumps up to greet him. He ruffles the dog and goes towards the gate that opens onto the alley. The dog thinks perhaps a* *walk is in the offing.* **Sharm** *pauses, glances back up to the bedroom window and sees that* **Uncle Sangi** *is looking out.* **Uncle Sangi** *smiles and waves.* **Sharm** *turns again to the gate.*

With sudden and fearsome uproar the yard door bursts open, and the neighbour kicks his way in. He is in a state of angry excitement, dragging the Devs' dustbin. He thrusts it into the yard and tips it over.

Neighbour: Here! keep the rubbish where it belongs. [*The dog is alarmed. Barks wildly.* **Sharm** *is bewildered*]

Neighbour: [*To the dog*] Shut up, you! Get on, get off! [*He aims a kick at the dog. The dog retaliates, and bites back. The* **Neighbour** *scrambles back into the alley howling with pain, and fright*]

Neighbour: Me leg, oh! me leg! [**Sharm** *rushes to the door, slams it shut, rams the bolt*]

Neighbour: [*Shouting*] Ye bloody savages! Oh, me leg, me leg. Me leg! [**Sharm** *looks up to* **Uncle Sangi**]

13   The passageway outside the living room

Sharm *is eavesdropping at the door. The voices of his mother and father are heard from inside the living room.*

Mr Dev: [*In Punjabi*] Explaining, I am explaining!

Mrs Dev: [*In Punjabi*] He is not understanding.

Mr Dev: [*In Punjabi*] I am explaining, Monday, Tuesday, Wednesday . . . .

14   The living room

Mr *and* **Mrs Dev** *are being interviewed by a* **Police**

Officer. *The* **Officer** *is impassive and bored. As the interview proceeds he is confirmed in his feeling of dislike for the Devs.*

Mr Dev: [*In English*] Thursday, Friday, Saturday, Sunday. [*Turning to the* **Officer**] I am saying, every day, I am working here. Only for ten minutes I go out ... what happens? 'Will Mr Dev please to come to the foyer, there is police message.'

Officer: That's life, isn't it?

Mr Dev: It is no life. I am horrified! I do not want my name called out in Jesmond Picture House.

Officer: But let's get back to the point, sir. Were you aware the dog had a vicious nature?

Mr Dev: Not even my dog.

Officer: Not your dog, sir?

Mr Dev: I did not bring it here. Come in off the street. The damn dog is English, but begging your pardon.

Officer: [*Coldly*] You have a licence, sir?

Mr Dev: Licence?

Officer: Dog licence.

Mr Dev: A dog needs papers? But I tell you I don't bring it from India.

Officer: No licence! [*Notes it down*]

Mrs Dev: Excuse me . . . . What does the law say?

Officer: The law says, you keep a dog, you must have a licence. You'll get a summons for that.

Mr Dev: Oh!

Officer: No bother. Just plead guilty by letter. Small fine.

Mr Dev: Oh!

Officer: But on the other hand, it *has* bitten your neighbour.

Mr Dev: I don't like it biting my neighbour.

Officer: He's not too happy about it either. You might find the law strange in this respect. If a dog bites another animal, say a sheep, or a horse, that's sufficient for a magistrate to make an order for control, or whatever. But if a dog bites a person, it is necessary for the victim to prove that the owner kept the dog, knowing it had a vicious tendency towards mankind.

Mr Dev: You mean in English law, it is wrong to bite animals, but not wrong to bite people?

Officer: Not quite, sir.

Mr Dev: I don't follow.

Officer: Has it bitten anyone before?

Mrs Dev: No. I don't think so.

Officer: You don't think so?

Mrs Dev: I am sure this is the first time.

Mr Dev: You mean, with people, it is allowed one bite?

Officer: Well, strangely, in a way ... yes. It's a matter of establishing a pattern of behaviour. Where people are involved, there are usually extenuating circumstances.

Mr Dev: I don't understand these kind of words.

Officer: Your son claims your neighbour broke in, and kicked the dog.

Mr Dev: My son very truthful.

Officer: On the other hand, your neighbour is quite insistent, he was simply putting your bin into your yard, when the dog attacked him.

Mr Dev: I would like to think my neighbour is also an honest man.

Officer: Now if there had been a witness.

Mr Dev: Witness?

Officer: Someone, who might have independently seen what happened. [**Mr** and **Mrs Dev** *exchange an anxious glance*] There wasn't anyone else present was there?

Mr Dev: Oh! no. No one else.

Officer: Pity. Well, it's a bit of a storm in a teacup. If I can smooth it out . . . .

Mr Dev: Can you do that? Oh! I would be most grateful.

Officer: Wasn't much of a bite.

Mr Dev: I'm so glad.

Officer: Hardly broke the skin.

Mr Dev: I am trusting he is fully recovered.

Officer: On the other hand, if he brings a private summons, we must go along with it.

Mr Dev: Oh dear!

Officer: You'd have to appear in court.

Mr Dev: [*The threat of court completely undermines him*] Oh, my God!

Officer: If it goes against you, you may be allowed to keep the dog, but as they say, 'at your peril'.

Mr Dev: I am not wishing to keep the dog anywhere.

Officer: [*Sighs*] But . . . see what we can do.

Mr Dev: Oh, please, that is very kind. You tell my neighbour I am very sorry he is bitten.

Officer: You could tell him yourself.

Mr Dev: Please, I think you will do it better.

Officer: Your son claims, he was called a black . . . you know, a black something or other.

Mr Dev: Oh, that is all right. I think it is all, how we say, in the heat of the moment. We are always telling him not to take any notice of that sort of thing.

Mrs Dev: We explain to him.

Mr Dev: Oh, yes, we explain.

Mrs Dev: In India we used to call European children, the little white monkeys.

Mr Dev: Oh no, no. I have never called anyone white monkey.

Mrs Dev: I am not saying you . . . .

Mr Dev: Never, never! Only very rude people say that. I have never called anyone white monkey, never.

Officer: Quite! [*He rises as a signal that the interview is over*]

Mrs Dev: Can we make you a cup of tea?

Officer: [*As though he'd been offered a five pound note*] No, thank you.

Mr Dev: You tell him I am very sorry. You tell him the dog will not bite him again.

Officer: I should hope not.

Mr Dev: Indeed no. It will be put down.

Officer: Put down?

Mr Dev: I will see to that. You tell him.

Officer: Well, it's your dog, sir.

Mr Dev: Oh, yes! I will not allow it. It will not cause any more trouble. It will be put down.

Officer: I see, sir! [*Just as they open the door of the living room,* **Sharm** *backs away from the door and runs upstairs in horror*]

15   Uncle Sangi's bedroom

Uncle Sangi *is packing his case.* **Sharm** *bursts in. He is greatly distressed.*

Sharm: Uncle Sangi! Uncle Sangi!

Sangi: Ssssh!

Sharm: [*Pulling wildly at* **Sangi's** *arm*] Come an' tell them. Tell them.

Sangi: [*Embraces* **Sharm**] Sssh! No.

Sharm: You got to tell them.

Sangi: Sharm! No! [*He places his hand across* **Sharm's** *mouth compelling him to silence.* **Sharm** *squirms but* **Sangi** *holds him firmly. Downstairs, there are the sounds of the* **Officer** *leaving.* **Mr Dev** *calls after him*]

Mr Dev: Goodbye, sir! And thank you again. And thank him he is shifting my bin for me. Goodbye, sir!

[**Sangi** *releases his grip of* **Sharm**]

Sharm: They're goin' to put him down, Uncle Sangi.

Sangi: All right, Sharm, all right.

Sharm: You can tell them.

Sangi: Sharm!

Sharm: Please, Uncle Sangi, please. He's a good dog. The man kicked him. You saw.

Sangi: Sharm!

Sharm: Please, Uncle Sangi.

Sangi: Sharm . . . I . . . .

Sharm: You like dogs.

Sangi: Sharm . . . I can't . . . speak.

Sharm: Why, Uncle Sangi? Why? [*They are almost in tears*]

Sangi: Oh, Christ! [*He sweeps his jacket from the top of his case. The pistol is revealed*]

Sharm: Uncle Sangi!

Sangi: Christ!

16   The passageway

Uncle Sangi *comes downstairs, bringing his case. He lays it on the hallstand table. He listens at the kitchen door.*

Mrs Dev: [*In the kitchen*]You know, I was thinking, maybe next week, before you go back to school, we could take a trip to Edinburgh. Lovely zoo there. You'd like that, eh? Well, a cheap day return is only three pound.

[**Uncle Sangi** *goes into the kitchen.* **Sharm** *is disconsolate before an uneaten breakfast.* **Mrs Dev** *is washing up at the sink*]

Sangi: [*In Punjabi*] Good morning!

Mrs Dev: [*In Punjabi*] Good morning.

Sangi: Sharm!

[**Sharm** *refuses to look up.* **Sangi** *and* **Mrs Dev** *exchange a glance*]

Mrs Dev: Your taxi was ordered for nine. Should be here any minute.

Sangi: Thank you. [*He attempts vainly to make contact with* **Sharm**]

Mrs Dev: Manjit is stocktaking.

Sangi: Oh!

Mrs Dev: It's all right. The shop's closed. Just go through!

Sangi: Yes. [*With a last glance at* **Sharm**, **Sangi** *makes his way to the shop door.* **Mrs Dev** *follows in order to close the door behind him. As he goes into the shop,* **Sangi** *speaks to* **Mr Dev**] Manjit!

Mr Dev: [*In the shop, in Punjabi*] You are nearly ready?

Sangi: [*In the shop*] Manjit!

Mr Dev: [*In Punjabi*] Just a moment.

[**Mrs Dev** *closes the door*]

17 The shop

Mr Dev *is stocktaking. He counts the tins and packets on the shelves, and marks his figures down on a clip board.*

Mr Dev: Just a moment. Seven by one dozen, six ounce, sage and onion.

Sangi: Manjit!

Mr Dev: Seventy-eight pence a dozen, seven eights, fifty-six.

Sangi: Manjit, I beg you, realize what is important.

Mr Dev: Seven sevens forty-nine, plus five . . . .

Sangi: You must not destroy that dog.

Mr Dev: [*Writing down figures*] Five pounds, forty-six. I need to concentrate, Sangi. Two dozen, three ounce, parsley sauce.

Sangi: Manjit!

Mr Dev: Thirty pence a dozen.

Sangi: You must not do it.

Mr Dev: [*Snapping into irritation*] It has been talked out.

Sangi: Think of your son.

Mr Dev: I think only of my son. It is only because I think of my son I do everything.

Sangi: You destroy his dog, you destroy him. You destroy justice.

Mr Dev: Justice! Sangi. I have matriculation standard of education. I have City and Guilds certificate, Civil Engineering, and I am counting damn packets of stuffing. Don't talk to me of justice.

Sangi: We are in England.

Mr Dev: Oh, yes, in England. Nowhere in the world is there so much justice. Nowhere is it more precious. So precious, they don't just give it away to anyone.

Sangi: An Englishman can hate your guts, but he will give you a place in the queue.

Mr Dev: Try asking, Sangi!

Sangi: It is not to be asked for, it is to be expected. But we must do more, Manjit. We must deserve it.

Mr Dev: A dog, Sangi, a damned dog!

Sangi: It is within ourselves. They are not killing the dog. We are killing the dog. They will not respect us for that.

Mr Dev: I am not going to court for a damned domestic animal. I am not drawing attention to myself. Look, if it was a wild dog, they would not be surprised it bites, but a domestic dog must never bite.

Sangi: Not even when it is kicked?

Mr Dev: Not even when it is kicked! There is a bad time coming, Sangi! Don't you realize, we must be careful.

Sangi: And is that the spirit of Punjab? Is it what you will teach your son?

Mr Dev: He will come to understand.

Sangi: He will understand that fear destroys justice.

Mr Dev: And you talk.

Sangi: Yes, it is true, I also am afraid.

Mr Dev: Some things we have to accept.

Sangi: If he does not find justice even in his own family . . . Manjit, I will speak out.

Mr Dev: You will do no such thing.

Sangi: Agree, and I will come forward.

Mr Dev: No.

Sangi: I will tell them.

Mr Dev: Tell them! Tell them what? That you have jumped your ship? That you are illegal immigrant? That you have mixed with petty criminals? Tell them you are crazy!

[*The doorbell rings*]

Sangi: Your son is despising me!

Mrs Dev: [*Entering*] Sangi, your taxi is here.

Sangi: [*Calling out*] Sharm! Sharm! [*He rushes out into the passageway*]

Mr Dev: Don't, Sangi!

Sangi: Sharm!

Mrs Dev: He has gone out.

Sangi: Out? [*He is trembling with emotion.* **Mr Dev** *takes hold of him*]

Mr Dev: Sangi! I am only destroying a dog. You would destroy us all.

[*The doorbell rings again.* **Sangi** *calms down.*

Mr Dev: Take your case, Sangi, and go now. [**Sangi's** *attention is drawn to his case, he notices the clasp is open. Upon a presentiment of something amiss,* **Sangi** *reaches for it*] Please, Sangi, leave us in peace. [**Sangi** *tears open his case, and frantically rummages around inside*] Sangi! What is it? [**Sangi** *turns and bolts to the door*]

Mr Dev: Sangi! [**Sangi** *seizes the astonished* **Taxi Driver** *who is standing at the door, and hustles him to the car*]

18   The dock road

The taxi pulls up next to the timber yards. **Uncle Sangi** *jumps out, and races across the road. The* **Driver** *steps out of his vehicle.*

Taxi Driver: Hey! man, hey!

Sangi: [*He blunders wildly across the waste ground calling out for* **Sharm.** *He searches the timber piles and clambers over obstacles. Out of breath, he pauses to scan the area*] Sharm! Sharm! [*He begins to run again. There is the report of a pistol shot.* **Sangi** *halts*] Sharm! [*He looks towards the sound of the shot.* **Sharm** *emerges from behind a timber stack. He looks towards his uncle. They stay motionless, then* **Sangi**

walks towards him. **Sharm** is holding the pistol]

Taxi Driver: [*Picking up his intercom*] Hello, Elsie! Charlie! Put us in a nine-nine, darlin'. Dock Road. Over.

Intercom Voice: Trouble, Charlie? Over.

Taxi Driver: Nothin' the law can't sort out.

[**Sangi** *and* **Sharm** *are within a few feet of each other. They come together in an embrace.*

The camera pulls away from them until they are mere specks on the riverscape]

The end

Short Back and Sides

Alan Plater

First broadcast in two parts by Yorkshire Television

Characters

John Hardy, a city planning officer
Carstairs, his senior assistant
Heather, local radio reporter
Dan, a barber
Beattie, landlady of a city centre pub
Nell, a customer in the pub
Gillian, Hardy's daughter
Withers, Chairman of the Planning Committee

John Hardy (played by Michael Bryant) in
Yorkshire Television's production of Short Back and
Sides.
Photograph by Brian Cleasby. Copyright © Trident
Television Ltd, 1976

Part I

---

1   An urban motorway complex

This is a jargonese description of the kind of spaghetti junction that can be found in most large cities, in most countries.

What we see first is a medium close shot of John Hardy. He is standing on a small patch of earth reserved for pedestrians. It is probably called an 'over-pass'. He is fortyish, dressed for a well-paid office job. He addresses the camera.

Hardy: And when my daughter says: 'What did you do to make the world a better place?' I shall say: 'Sweetheart – I made this!'

[*There is a roar of traffic as he turns his head and waves his hand in the direction of what he has made. The camera pans to a wide shot of the motorways in action: cars and lorries and assorted juggernauts and not a child, not a corner shop, not a flower to be seen anywhere*]

2   Hardy's office

Hardy *sits at his desk in an office befitting a county planning officer in one of the new metropolitan counties: it is very smart, verging on the plush. In* *addition to the desk and chair there is a drawing board, plans on the wall, rolls of drawings, a large cabinet for the storage of drawings, plus one or two personal belongings that go slightly against the official grain such as a picture of Buster Keaton.*

There is a tap on the door, which then opens and **Carstairs** *comes in. He is a bright and ambitious man in his mid-thirties – not all that posh. He places a small stack of files on* **Hardy's** *desk.* **Hardy** *tries to suppress a giggle.*

Carstairs: I'm sorry . . . ?

Hardy: No. *I'm* sorry . . . it's my fault. [*He picks up the top file*] I know you're my senior assistant and very highly qualified, but I can't help thinking your name is Carstairs and I know it isn't your fault but every time you walk in fresh in the morning; I want to say: 'What ho, Carstairs?' [*Pause*] Is that terrible?

Carstairs: I can think of worse things.

Hardy: I feel we ought to bring these things into the open, rather than let them fester and spoil a good working relationship. [*All the time he is browsing through the files*] What is all this garbage?

Carstairs: The agenda for next week's committee meeting. It's mostly people wanting to build greenhouses and verandahs and we are saying, yes, they may . . . .

Hardy: Tomatoes and cucumbers will flourish and grow over all the earth. [*He picks up another, fatter file*] This is a fat one.

Carstairs: Phase Three.

Hardy: Phase Three of the city's Integrated Transport System. [*Opens the file and reads*] All Saints.

Carstairs: We might have a little trouble.

Hardy: Not on the committee.

Carstairs: No, not on the committee.

Hardy: The Conservatives will support it because they supported Phase One. The Labour Party will support it because they supported Phase Two. So they'll both support Phase Three. Carried unanimously and good night nurse. Good things, six lane motorways . . . the ratepayers can see what they're getting for their money.

Carstairs: I gather it's the people who live in All Saints.

Hardy: Ah. The voice of the people, your favourite and mine.

Carstairs: People don't like being demolished.

Hardy: I'm giving a lecture to the Civic Society this evening. I'm taking part in a phone-in programme on local radio tomorrow . . . how far can participation go? [*He closes the file*] People don't mind being demolished if you can prove they voted for it.

3   Lecture room

Hardy *is giving his lecture to the civic society.*

Hardy: I am your city planning officer. Every city planning officer thinks he is misunderstood. We have that in common with the rest of the human race. In other words, if you prick me, do I not complain . . . ? The answer is yes I do, though I do try to whistle and smile under all difficulties. First slide, please. [*Slide 1: Map of the City*] Plan of the city, vintage 1960. Lovely city, designed for horse-drawn vehicles. Message to city planning officer from the people:

design a city for motor cars. Next slide please. [*Slide 2: Map of the City with inner ring road drawn on in red – just a big red circle, savage in its implications*] We build an inner ring road. Integrated transport scheme, Phase One. Next slide please. [*Slide 3: Same map plus an outer ring road – a bigger red circle*] Phase Two. An outer ring road. Next slide please. [*Slide 4: same with the two red circles linked by a series of connecting loops: all now like a plate of spaghetti*] Phase Three. The integrated transport scheme is now complete . . . or it will be when we build Phase Three. [*Pause*] The problem is that the same people who want room to drive their motor cars can get sentimental about losing well-loved churches, chapels, public houses, corner shops, public conveniences of Gothic proportions, alleyways with tender memories of teenage romance and institutions of that kind. Next slide please. [*Slide 5: Venice – a view of gondolas on a canal*] If we travelled by gondola there would be no problem. Our city would look like this. Next slide please. [*Slide 6: motorway shambles – a picture similar to the opening film sequence*] But we don't travel by gondola. We travel by motor car. What you see is the vision of what we desire . . . if you'll forgive the expression.

4   Radio studio

Small local radio studio. **Hardy** *sits at a table with a young radio reporter called* **Heather**; *she's bright and resourceful. The studio is equipped for a phone-in programme.*

Heather: And our studio guest is John Hardy, the city planning officer, and the subject for discussion is

Phase Three of the city's integrated transport scheme, especially as it affects the All Saints area of the city . . . your phone-in line is double-two, double-three, one, have we any callers on the line? [*Pause*]

Hardy: Please don't worry if nobody wants to talk to me. I'm quite used to it.

Heather: Anyway, while we're waiting . . . .

Hardy: [*Breaks in*] While we're waiting, perhaps I could choose a record? I've always wanted to choose a record . . . . My daughter would like the second movement from Mozart's Eine Kleine Nachtmusik, I'd like anything by Miles Davis, and there's a chap at work called Carstairs, but I think he prefers a good book. [*Pause*] I'm sorry, am I talking too much?

Heather: No, that's perfectly all right, Mr Hardy . . . .

Hardy: Just it must be a bit embarrassing having a phone-in with somebody that nobody wants to talk to. So let's get the record straight. I'm not embarrassed.

Heather: Good. And just to remind listeners, our studio guest is John Hardy, city planning officer, and your phone-in line is double-two, double-three, one . . . .

[*A light flashes to indicate there's a caller on the line*]

Hardy: There's a light flashing on your desk, did you know?

Heather: Indeed there is, and that means we have our first caller on the line . . . . [*She picks up the phone.* **Hardy** *listens in on headphones*] Can you give me your name, caller?

[*The caller's name is* **Dan**, *though we don't know this yet*]

Dan: [*His voice is distorted by the phone*] This is the demon barber of All Saints.

Heather: The . . . ?

Dan: [*Distorted*] The demon barber of All Saints.

Hardy: You can't fool me. That's Carstairs, isn't it?

Dan: [*Distorted*] Your name's Hardy, is that right?

Hardy: That's right. Hardy by name and hardy by nature.

Dan: Another fine mess you've got us into, Mr Hardy. [*The line goes dead*]

Hardy: That was quite a short conversation wasn't it?

Heather: Yes, it was rather.

Hardy: What shall we do now? Quick flash of the Eine Kleine Nachtmusik?

5   A pub

It is a small, frieldly, old-fashioned, working-class pub. We see **Dan** *standing beside a coin-operated phone close by the bar. He is in his late fifties and has seen it all. He laughs.*

There is another burst of laughter in response and we see **Beattie**, *the landlady, behind the bar: she's small but tough, and smiles without fear. Leaning on the bar is* **Nell**: *she's a jolly woman who might be persuaded to sell kisses to a nice sailor.*

Dan: That's enough participation for one day.

Beattie: Won't make no difference though, will it?

Nell: Never does.

6 Hardy's living room

Hardy *and his daughter,* **Gillian,** *who is seventeen – taking A-levels, and will probably get distinctions in everything. She is doing her homework.* **Hardy** *is sprawled in an armchair doodling on a large sketch pad. The room is decorated and furnished in modern style without being flash, and overlaid with personal idiosyncrasies: posters from a long-ago exhibition, LP sleeves, fragment of an old loom, etc. It is a lived-in and used room.*

Gillian: Have you really done what the man said?

Hardy: Yes, I did it. But I was insane, I got the red mist in front of my eyes . . . what are you talking about?

Gillian: Got us into another fine mess.

Hardy: You were listening?

Gillian: I always listen to our friendly neighbourhood radio station . . . I keep hoping they'll play the Eine Kleine Nachtmusik . . . .

Hardy: The trouble with phone-in programmes is the only people who phone in are the sort of people who phone in . . . .

Gillian: To phone-in programmes.

Hardy: Precisely. And he wouldn't have said that about another fine mess if my name wasn't Hardy. [*Pause*] Could have been worse. He could have said: kiss me. [*Pause*]

Gillian: You laughed at him.

Hardy: He described himself as the demon barber of All Saints. I reckon he was laughing at himself to start with . . . .

Gillian: But you do laugh at people.

Hardy: I've got a senior assistant called Carstairs . . . I've got a committee chairman who sells dustbins for a living . . . I spend half my professional life giving permission for people to turn disused chapels into cut-price wallpaper emporiums . . . emporia? You've got to laugh, sweetheart . . . either that or an overdose.

Gillian: It's too easy.

Hardy: I read in a dentist's waiting room that you use more muscles to frown than to smile . . . or was it the other way about?

Gillian: So what?

Hardy: That's what I thought at the time. I think there was a moral to it. Frown and stay fit. Smile and go sloppy. What's your homework?

Gillian: History.

Hardy: [*Crosses to look*] That's a relief. I thought maybe it was A-level Potted Psychology . . . all about laughter as a way of protecting yourself against the pain of everyday life . . . .

Gillian: Dear mother . . . father's going round the twist . . . .

Hardy: Please send money and tranquillizers . . . .

Gillian: No, it's only history.

Hardy: That old thing.

Gillian: You remember Tony?

Hardy: Tony?

Gillian: That spotty youth, that's what you called him.

Hardy: Yes, I remember Tony. Spotty youth. He

wanted you to run away with him and start a traditional folk group.

Gillian: When I telephoned him to say 'Sorry, Tony, I
don't want to see you again . . .' it was quite easy . . .
because I couldn't see his face. I think he was crying
but I couldn't see the tears, so it didn't worry me.

Hardy: You did a phone-in job on him.

Gillian: Right.

Hardy: Face to face with people's tears. That can be
difficult.

[*Pause*]

Gillian: Before you decided to drive a motorway
through All Saints, did you go and look at the area?

Hardy: Of course. We called it a comprehensive
survey . . . we went and looked at it . . . .

Gillian: Did you get out of your car?

[*Pause.* **Hardy** *picks up one of the books she is
studying*]

Hardy: Tom Paine.

Gillian: [*Deliberately parrot-fashion*] Thomas Paine,
1737 to 1809 . . . he said . . . Government, even in its
best state, is a necessary evil: in its worst state, an
intolerable one. [*Pause*] He would have got out of his
car to see if the people were crying.

7 'All Saints' area of the city

*It is a decent, somewhat down-at-heel, working-class
area, thrown up in the late nineteenth century, rather*

like the sort of scene often painted by Lowry. **Hardy** *is walking along the street. Beyond him we see his small car parked.*

8   The pub (It is the pub we saw in scene 5)

Beattie *is behind the counter.* **Nell** *sits in her favourite corner. The place is otherwise deserted.* **Hardy** *enters and crosses to bar.*

Hardy: Afternoon.

Beattie: Afternoon, dear . . . .

Hardy: Draught lager, please.

Beattie: Pint?

Hardy: Half, please. Driving my car.

Nell: Lucky feller.

Hardy: Lucky?

Beattie: You've got a big car.

Hardy: How do you know it's a big one?

Beattie: Got a clue from the way you talk. You talk like a feller that's got a big car.

Nell: And the suit.

Beattie: Not a fifty-shilling suit, that one. Suit that goes with a big car. [*She pulls the drink for* **Hardy**] Got another clue from looking through that window. Saw you arrive. Saw you get out of your big car.

Hardy: That really was shrewd.

Beattie: I'm often complimented on my shrewdness.

[*She gives him his drink. He pays for it, all in silence.* **Hardy** *feels, correctly, that he is being weighed up. Eventually he breaks the silence*]

Hardy: It's . . . quiet.

Beattie: Aye, it is.

Nell: Very quiet.

Beattie: Very slack.

Hardy: Trade's slack?

Beattie: Well . . . look at it. [*They look at the empty pub*]

Nell: Not doing the balance of payments any good is it?

Beattie: No good at all.

Nell: And we're willing to help . . . .

Hardy: What? Help the balance of payments?

Beattie: Overseas customers welcome.

Nell: I like Norwegians.

Beattie: English spoken.

Nell: Very gentle, somehow, the Norwegians.

Beattie: But if nobody turns up, what can you do?

Hardy: Where have they all gone?

Nell: [*Laughing*] Norway I suppose.

Hardy: Customers. In general, whatever their race.

Beattie: Where have all the customers gone?

Nell: Same place as the flowers. Where have all the flowers gone . . . .

Beattie: They've run away. Trying to beat the bulldozers.

Hardy: Are the bulldozers coming?

Beattie: Say you're a flower . . . you don't wait for the bulldozer. The threat's enough. You pull up your roots and run.

Nell: Don't hang about.

Beattie: Else you get mown down. Phase Three.

Hardy: [*Reacts*] Phase Three?

Beattie: I used to think I lived at number seven, Station Street, All Saints . . . but I don't.

Nell: We live in Phase Three.

Beattie: There was a feller on the wireless talking about it. Didn't understand what he was on about except we live in Phase Three.

Nell: Dan the barber rang him up. Played hell with him.

Hardy: Who's Dan the barber?

Beattie: His name's Dan . . . and . . . .

Hardy: [*Breaks in*] I bet he's a barber.

Nell: Thought you didn't know him.

Hardy: I guessed.

Beattie: Shrewd.

Hardy: I'm often complimented on my shrewdness.

Nell: Bet you've got a big car an' all . . . .

Hardy: Enormous. [*Pause*] So he's a barber, this man? Cuts hair? That sort of thing?

Beattie: Scissors and a comb.

Nell: And a pudding basin. Does a good haircut. Last you for months.

Beattie: And if he gives you a shave they reckon it lasts for ever. [*Everyone smiles*]

9 The 'All Saints' area

Hardy *makes his way across a piece of waste ground – past the remains of sheds. There is graffiti on*

corrugated iron. A horse is tethered on some waste land.
Hardy *stops.*

He is looking at **Dan** *the barber's: an old-fashioned corner shop at the end of a terrace, with a red and white pole.* **Hardy** *goes in.*

10   Inside the barber's shop

Hardy *enters.* **Dan** *is sitting in the chair, reading a racing paper. The place is small, and none too clean.*

There is a bench for waiting customers, littered with old newspapers and magazines: on the walls, there are advertisements for haircream that no longer exists and photographs of almost-forgotten professional boxers and of hair-styles with centre partings gummed down with Brylcreem.

Dan *doesn't turn as* **Hardy** *enters but hears the slightly cracked sound of the bell on the door, and gives a casual glance via the tarnished mirror.*

Dan: Now then.

Hardy: Er . . . now then.

Dan: Where do you want to be?

Hardy: I don't want to be anywhere special . . . .

Dan: Mostly the people who come in here are lost. They come in to ask the way to somewhere.

Hardy: I know exactly where I am. The parish of All Saints. Dan the barber's, to be absolutely precise.

Dan: And there's nothing like being absolutely precise. [*Gets up to have a closer look at* **Hardy**, *who sits down on the bench*] Absolute precision. Good thing to have, is that. [*Pause*] You're not a customer are you?

Hardy: Why not?

Dan: You don't look like my sort of customer. You look more like the sort of feller that goes to a gentleman's hair stylist. A salon.

Hardy: And this is something different?

Dan: This is a barber's. You saw the red and white pole? Historically speaking, we used to be blood-letters. Don't get much of that these days. Don't get much of anything. But yon's the chair if you fancy it . . . . [**Hardy** *looks at the chair. Cautiously, he crosses the room and sits down. The chair creaks a little as he pivots on it.* **Dan** *inspects the back of his neck*] Short back and sides, is it?

Hardy: What does that consist of, precisely?

Dan: With absolute precision, sir, it consists of a haircut that is short at the back and short at the sides. Used to give them to little lads the day before they went back to school after the summer holidays. There you are, son, I'd say . . . that'll keep you going till Christmas. And it did.

Hardy: I generally have a light trim.

Dan: A light trim. [*He weighs the words and the implications*] I'm not sure I've got the tools for a light trim. [*He picks up the scissors and the hand-clippers from his bench. They seem fairly primitive*] I'm not sure I've got the background either. It's all a matter of background. Experience. Breeding. I mean, I'm game, I'll have a go . . . .

Hardy: What about a shave?

Dan: That's a pleasing thought. I'm in training for that. [*He runs his fingers over* **Hardy's** *chin*] I bet you use electric.

Hardy: Yes. It's quick and it's clean and it's . . . .

Dan: [*Breaking in*] And it's useless . . . you've got a light beard, sir, but it feels like a doormat. . . . [*He runs his fingers over his own chin*] Whereas that . . . it's like a baby's bum. [*He starts to strop his old-fashioned razor*] Aye, I'll give you a shave you won't forget. [*As the sequence proceeds, he shaves* **Hardy**]

Hardy: Have you been in business long?

Dan: Twenty, thirty years.

Hardy: You must have seen a few changes.

Dan: That's what royalty say.

Hardy: Is it?

Dan: Whenever royalty's being shown round some place on one of their tours . . . say a cement works or a saucepan factory . . . royalty always gets introduced to somebody that's worked there longer than anybody else . . . and she always says 'You must have seen a few changes . . . .'

Hardy: Well, I promise you, I'm not royalty.

Dan: No, you don't get them coming to All Saints. Somebody came in the war, when we got bombed. That was the bombsite you walked across to get here. Aye. Somebody came when we got bombed. Not royalty though. Was it Churchill? It might have been. I can't remember. If they'd said, 'You must have seen some changes', we could have said, 'Yes, we have, we just had all our houses bombed.' But I don't suppose they'd ask the question. Not in that situation.

Hardy: I'd still be interested to hear about the changes.

Dan: Certainly, your majesty. Well . . . [*And he goes into his story integrating it into his shaving routine –*

like any barber being sociable with his customer]
When I first came here it was a traditional, old-
fashioned working-class community. Everybody
worked hard at the mill. Everybody played hard.
Drank their pints. Whippet racing and pigeon racing
and bare-knuckle contests back of the Weavers Arms
every night at closing time. Area Championships on
a Saturday night. If you were in the know, there was
cock-fighting and bear-baiting. Baked our own bread.
Built our own simple dwellings. Every August the
gypsies would gather on the common to trade their
horses. And whenever a stranger wandered into our
midst, we'd break bread with him and tell him tales,
and give him the best shave he'd ever had in his life.

[*Pause*]

Hardy: What about the substandard housing
conditions?

Dan: The rats and the mice and the cockroaches and
the outside lavatories?

Hardy: That kind of thing.

Dan: Got plenty of those. There's everything under
this floor, do you know that? There's vermin under
this floor they haven't got names for . . . . [*More con-
fidential*] Some fellers came from the University and
took samples of the vermin droppings . . . from under
this floor . . . they went back to their laboratories and
their test-tubes and after a year's work they're going
to invent names for all the hitherto unidentified
vermin. [*Pause*] And then we'll have a place in the
history books.

Hardy: Something to be proud of?

Dan: It's a kind of distinction, isn't it? Whichever

way you look at it. Hey, have you seen my calendar? [*He draws* **Hardy's** *attention to a calendar hanging on the wall.* **Hardy** *has to twist his head slightly to see it and almost catches his neck on the open razor*] Steady.

Hardy: Sorry.

Dan: Could have lost your head then.

Hardy: I was trying to see your calendar.

Dan: What would your wife have said?

Hardy: She said I'd lose it one day. [*The calendar has a large picture at the top – a landscape by Constable: Flatford Mill. It is very English*] Yes, it's a nice calendar. John Constable.

Dan: The master of English landscape. You look at that . . . you see the trees and the grass and the sky and you can hear the running of water and the singing of the birds . . . .

Hardy: Pastoral.

Dan: Oh, aye. Pastoral all right. Highly pastoral. Tell you something else.

Hardy: What?

Dan: What you see on that picture . . . if you went there . . . you'd find it was alive with rats and mice and creepy-crawlies nobody's invented a name for . . . take the trees away and there's not a lot of difference between Constable's England and under my floorboards. [*Pause*] And nobody's going to go *there* . . . . [*Pointing his razor at the picture*] . . . and say, hey up, you're Phase Three, we're going to drive a damn great motorway through the middle of your mill . . . . [*The shave is now completed. With a towel* **Dan** *dries* **Hardy's** *chin*] Aye . . . another fine mess.

Hardy: Feels all right to me. Like a baby's bottom.

Dan: I've got some pansy-smelling stuff here in a bottle.... [**Dan** *picks up a small bottle from a shelf*] I didn't buy it, like. Traveller left it. Sample. [*He unscrews the top and sniffs it*] Fancy a splash?

Hardy: Why not? [**Dan** *applies the after-shave.* **Hardy** *grimaces*]

Dan: You'll get lots of exciting new friends if you wear this, I believe.

Hardy: It stings a bit.

Dan: It stings a bit but you get used to it. Just like life, wouldn't you say, sir?

Hardy: It could well be.

Dan: There we are. [*He removes the cloth from* **Hardy** *who stands up and inspects himself in the mirror*] A shave that befits your status.

Hardy: Thank you. [*He turns to* **Dan**] How much do I owe you?

Dan: And that's quite a profound question an' all... wouldn't you say? Sir?

11 Hardy's living room

Hardy *and* **Gillian** *have met in the doorway,* **Gillian** *on her way in from school,* **Hardy** *in the process of setting the table. She has caught a whiff of the after-shave.*

Gillian: You smell like....

Hardy: [*Breaks in*] Thank you, I've already been told what I smell like....

Gillian: What is it?

Hardy: The official line is that it's a trade sample . . . my theory is that it was brewed by gypsies under the floorboards . . . distilled from the essence of old strong ale and pigeon droppings . . . .

Gillian: I don't understand.

Hardy: Are we meant to understand? That's quite a profound question, wouldn't you say, madam? [*Pause*]

Gillian: A beard would smell better than that. [*She moves off to hang up her coat*]

12 Hardy's office

Hardy *sits at his desk. There is a knock at the door.*

Hardy: Come in. [**Carstairs** *enters with a load of files and a roll of drawings.* **Hardy** *says quietly*] What ho. [**Carstairs** *gets a whiff of the smell and reacts, though he tries to conceal it*] I know, I smell.

Carstairs: You do a bit.

Hardy: I've tried washing it off but it clings.

Carstairs: It often does.

Hardy: Yes. Tried washing it off but it clings. [*He looks up at* **Carstairs**] Just like life, wouldn't you say, Carstairs?

13 The motorway complex

Hardy *looks into the camera.*

Hardy: Sweetheart – I made this!

[*Fade out*]

End of Part I

Part II

---

14 The urban motorway complex

Traffic streams along the motorways.

15 Hardy's living room

Gillian *is at the table, homework spread all around her.*
Hardy *is at the window. Music is coming from the*
record player. **Hardy** *crosses to the table.*

Hardy: Homework?

Gillian: You can't build a career without A-levels.

Hardy: What sort of career?

Gillian: I don't know. I haven't built it yet. Something useful.

Hardy: So . . . what sort of doctor are you going to be,
sweetheart?

Gillian: I mean, what do people need? Food, shelter,
water . . . .

Hardy: Food? You could be a farmer . . . .

Gillian: Allergic to pigs.

Hardy: Shelter . . . you could be a steel erector . . . .

Gillian: Thou shalt not steal.

Hardy: OK. You'll have to be a water diviner. [*He picks up one of her books*] History again?

Gillian: You can't do A-levels in water divining.

Hardy: Tom Paine?

Gillian: No. The Peasants' Revolt.

Hardy: The peasants are revolting.

Gillian: Dear mother . . . father's not only going round the twist, he's also turning into a fascist . . . .

Hardy: Many of my best friends are peasants . . . bare-knuckle fighters and gypsy horsetraders and demon barbers who were blood-letters in origin, I'll have you know . . . hence the red and white pole . . . .

Gillian: [*Still addressing 'mother'*] I'm trying to do my history and he keeps jabbering in my ear about blood-letting . . . .

Hardy: I'll tell you about history, my love . . . do you mind? [*He clears her books away to one side of the table, leaving a clear space end to end*] Over here . . . . [*At one end of the table*] . . . is where history starts . . . dinosaurs and other primaeval monsters fresh from the slime . . . enormous bodies and tiny brains and thick as two short planks . . . that's pre-history, right?

Gillian: Right.

Hardy: And over here . . . . [*The other end of the table*] . . . is the future . . . twenty-five thousand AD . . . man has colonized the planets . . . leisure centres on Mars . . . discount warehouses on Saturn . . . filling stations with treble stamps on Venus . . . you've got the picture?

Gillian: Dinosaurs . . . discount warehouses . . . . [*She indicates either end of the table*]

Hardy: On Saturn . . . the discount warehouses . . . .

Gillian: I know.

Hardy: Right. Somewhere here there's a speck of dust
. . . you can't see it it's so small . . . . [*He points to
invisible speck of dust*]

Gillian: You're right. It's so small I can't see it. [*She
peers at 'it'*] What is it?

Hardy: Phase Three of the integrated Transport
Scheme. All Saints. [*He blows it*] See. It's gone.

Gillian: The way of the dinosaurs.

16   Hardy's office

Hardy *and* **Carstairs** *are poring over a large road plan
which we identify as Phase Three – if only because the
words are written on in large letters.*

Hardy: Honest opinion, Carstairs?

Carstairs: Yes?

Hardy: All this lot. All these mighty roadworks and
underpasses and overpasses and roundabouts and
swings . . . is it important?

Carstairs: It's costing millions of pounds.

Hardy: That wasn't the question. What I said was . . .
is it important?

Carstairs: Of course it's important.

Hardy: Today, this minute, we haven't got all these
mighty roadworks . . . they're just lines on paper and
words in a report . . . and the sun rose this morning
without any trouble, and the birds still sang and the
milk arrived on the doorstep same as usual . . . he even

remembered the yoghurt . . . not that we ordered it, but still . . . .

Carstairs: With respect, I don't really know what you're talking about . . . .

Hardy: When people say: with respect, it generally means, without respect. With respect, sir, you're out of your mind . . . we've spent ten years preparing this marvellous road-building programme, we've employed all the best computers and all the latest information and now you tell me you're going out of your mind, sir. [*Pause*] Think about the broad sweep of history, Carstairs. The peasants' revolt. Blood-letting, food, shelter, water . . . . Supposing I've decided that seen alongside the broad sweep of history, Phase Three is a waste of time, money and effort . . . supposing I recommend to the committee that it's a load of nonsense and we should spend the money on something sensible?

Carstairs: I should think they'd ask for your resignation.

Hardy: For getting them into another fine mess . . . yes, I imagine they would. [*Pause*] You'd be all right. You're next in line.

Carstairs: I still don't see why you . . . .

Hardy: [*Breaking in as he hesitates*] Why I'm going round the bend? Well now . . . . [*He indicates the length of the drawing board on which the plans are displayed*] Imagine that's the broad sweep of history, Carstairs . . . . [**Carstairs** *looks*] Over here . . . there's a tiny speck of dust, so small you can't see it . . . . [**Carstairs** *looks at the tiny speck of dust at one end of the board*] That speck of dust is a dinosaur. ·

Carstairs: What ho, dinosaur.

17   The living room

Hardy *is doing a drawing of* **Gillian** *on a large sketch pad. She is posing, fairly casually. He draws quickly, approximately and well.*

Hardy: Carstairs is human. There's hope for humanity.

Gillian: Guess what I saw written on a wall today?

Hardy: Carstairs is human, OK?

Gillian: Wrong.

Hardy: Mrs Kilroy was here.

Gillian: No.

[*Pause*]

Hardy: Do I get another go?

Gillian: Yes.

Hardy: I didn't realize it was a three-part question . . . er . . . water-diviners bootboys aggro . . . .

Gillian: No. I went for a walk around All Saints. On a wall it said . . . 'Another fine mess . . . Hardy must go . . . .'

Hardy: Where was that?

Gillian: On a wall . . . near a barber's shop . . . .

Hardy: Dan the barber's . . . I know it well . . . .

Gillian: You don't.

Hardy: I never go anywhere else for my short back and sides . . . last you till Christmas . . . . [*He tears the drawing off the pad – not because he's displeased, but because he wants to write on the next sheet.* **Gillian** *looks at the drawing while he writes*] There was something I always wanted to write on a wall but

I never had enough paint or enough wall . . . .

Gillian: Let me guess . . . I love Mary Pickford . . . . True?

Hardy: I'm not that old.

Gillian: I hate Douglas Fairbanks. True.

Hardy: There. [*He reads it, and we see it written in large capitals on the drawing pad*] That which gives our dreams their daring is that they *can* be realized . . . .'

Gillian: [*Looks at it*] Explain.

Hardy: A man called Le Corbusier said that . . . an architect and a town planner.

Gillian: 'That which gives our dreams their daring is that they *can* be realized.'

Hardy: He meant that the only sort of dreams and visions that were worth having were brave ones . . . and what made them really brave was that we could make them happen . . . knock everything down and start again . . . build beautiful cities, starting from square one . . . like the song says . . . I'll knock you down, dirty old town . . . .

Gillian: Nothing wrong with that if you're clever enough.

Hardy: If you're clever enough. [*Pause*] I had dreams enough to stretch from here to Venus and Mars . . . but I had to work myself into a position to realize the dreams. Pass the examinations . . . brilliant degree . . . dazzling academic career . . . shot through the planning department like a meteor . . . the youngest chief planning officer in the land . . . .

Gillian: And the most handsome.

Hardy: Let's not put it to the vote.

Gillian: So . . . ? You're the best in the business . . . .

Hardy: So . . . on the day you were born I was being interviewed for a job . . . on your first birthday I was at a conference in Cambridge . . . on the day you started school I was on a fact-finding mission in Germany . . . you grew up and I never noticed . . . . I was always going to take you to feed the ducks tomorrow . . . but there was always a telephone call and somebody to see and we never ever got to feed the ducks and . . . .

[*Pause*]

Gillian: And?

Hardy: You know.

Gillian: That's why your wife and my mother found another bloke.

Hardy: That's why.

Gillian: I don't blame her.

Hardy: Thank you.

Gillian: I don't blame you.

Hardy: Thank you.

Gillian: Most people never have any dreams at all . . . .

Hardy: George Bernard Shaw . . . he said it . . . 'the true artist will let his wife starve, his children go barefoot . . . sooner than work at anything but his art . . . .'

[*They both realize* **Gillian** *is barefoot*]

Gillian: This is from choice.

Hardy: And there's no art in demolition. No art in the internal combustion engine. No dreams, my love . . . . I've spent millions of pounds and not a dream in sight . . . . [*Pause*] Got my chairman coming to see me tomorrow.

Gillian: Didn't realize you had your very own chairman.

Hardy: Chairman of the Planning Committee . . . Councillor Withers, the voice of the people . . . he's a very important man.

Gillian: Proof?

Hardy: The voters elected him.

Gillian: I still don't accept he's important. I want more proof.

Hardy: He's got the largest chain of hardware shops in the county . . . everybody uses his dustbins . . . .

Gillian: All right. He's important. Why is he coming to see you?

Hardy: Because I'm breaking rule number one . . . the thing that important people in public life should never, never do . . . .

Gillian: What rule number one?

Hardy: Never admit you were wrong.

Gillian: And you're admitting you were wrong?

Hardy: I cannot tell a lie. When I go to the great Chairman in the Sky I shall say: I was wrong.

Gillian: What about your Great Chairman in the Office? The dustbin king . . . .

Hardy: Oh. He'll probably say . . . .

18 The office: a flash forward

Withers: Have you considered all the implications . . . ?

19   The living room

Hardy: And I'll say, yes, I've considered most of the implications, let's say the thirty-seven most obvious ones, and he'll say . . . .

20   The office: another flash forward in time

Withers: Have you considered taking a holiday?

21   The living room

Hardy: And I'll say Majorca's too hot and Scarborough's too misty and my passport's out of date . . . .

Gillian: And then he'll say . . . .

Hardy: 'Let's get down to the nitty-gritty.' He always does that in the end, after the preliminary sparring.

22   The office

Withers: I think we should get down to the nitty-gritty.

Hardy: Why not? Long as it's not too gritty.

Withers: I mean, with respect, the only fault I've ever found with you is you tend to laugh too much . . . laugh at things that seem to me to be serious . . . like, well, spending ratepayers' money . . . so I'm asking you . . . are you really serious now?

Hardy: I am really serious. I am recommending to the Planning Committee that we scrap Phase Three of the Integrated Transport Scheme.

Withers: We'll be a laughing stock.

Hardy: No. Not you. *I'll* be a laughing stock. But that doesn't worry me . . . I like to hear people laughing . . . .

Withers: I doubt whether the committee will take your advice.

Hardy: That's all right. If the committee wants to carry on, that's their affair. I'll quietly resign . . . .

Withers: You intend to resign?

Hardy: If I think what my department's doing is a load of nonsense, I can hardly *not* resign. Be like a Jewish vegetarian running a pork butcher's . . . . [*Pause*] Sorry, I didn't mean to be offensive to pork butchers or . . . .

Withers: Are you sure you wouldn't like to take a holiday? You could have leave of absence . . . .

Hardy: There's nothing wrong with me, Mr Withers. I used to believe in one thing and then one day I had a shave and I stopped believing in it. It can happen to anybody. It happened to a feller I knew on the road to Damascus.

Withers: I don't know it.

Hardy: Probably you wouldn't. It's in Lancashire.

[*Pause*]

Withers: What will you do? If you resign?

Hardy: When I resign.

Withers: Presumably you'll go away and build roads for somebody else . . . a man with your qualifications.

Hardy: I think I'll just hang around street corners for a while . . . take my daughter to the park and feed the ducks, while the park's still there . . . .

Withers: [*Seeing a picture of* **Gillian** *on the desk*] How old's your daughter?

Hardy: Seventeen. I missed feeding the ducks at the proper time. I was at a conference, building a dazzling career. That's the trouble with the world ... everybody building dazzling careers and the ducks starve to death . . . not to mention the daughters . . . .

Withers: Look, it's not really my business but . . . .

Hardy: I might even procreate . . . .

Withers: I beg your pardon . . . ?

Hardy: Make another daughter. Or another son. Carry on with the non-existent family business. I cannot tell a lie, Mr Chairman . . . I have no resident wife. Nor even a resident woman. There have been momentary excitements but . . . I suppose I could obtain one . . . . Usual sources. Put a little ad in the Post Office window.

[*Pause*]

Withers: Have you considered seeing a doctor?

Hardy: The last time I saw my doctor I recognized him quite distinctly at a range of twenty yards, so I concluded there was nothing wrong with my eyesight.

Withers: [*Losing control*] Mr Hardy!

Hardy: [*Topping* **Withers's** *volume*] Mr Chairman! [*Pause*] There is no truth in the rumour that I am a loony. Look at this. [*He brings out a large photograph of the motorway development. A still of the area we saw in opening film sequence*] That's Phase Two. Phase Three is just the same but bigger and louder and smellier and even more expensive. I'm saying I don't believe in that as a dream any more. I'm saying it's a rotten dream and I was a fool ever to believe it.

Look at it. [*He forces* **Withers** *to look at it*] Where's the space for the old man's greenhouse? And the prizefighters and the horse-trading and the vermin, yes, let's not forget the vermin, they've got a place in the scheme of things as well. One man's vermin is another man's miracle of Nature. So – where is it? What happens to the lady who sells kisses to gentle Norwegians? And Dan the barber? And the neighbourhood water diviner? [*Pause*] All I'm saying is: I was wrong.

Withers: All I'm saying is: you should see a doctor.

[*Pause*]

Hardy: [*Quiet, thoughtful*] Anybody who admits he was wrong should see a doctor. [*Another pause*] Well . . . it's a point of view, Mr Chairman.

23   The living room

Hardy *sits in his living room. He is being interviewed for local radio by* **Heather**, *whom we met earlier. A little tape recorder is on a low table in front of them while* **Heather** *brandishes the mike. Beyond them,* **Gillian** *is looking and listening. As the interview proceeds she reacts.*

Heather: What made you resign, Mr Hardy?

Hardy: In two sentences?

Heather: As many as you like.

Hardy: Well . . . you can always edit it down to two . . . no, what it was . . . there was this feller . . . and he said I was going to make another fine mess . . . and I looked at what I had done and I said: it is a mess.

Heather: You're saying the Council's policy for the last ten years has been misguided?

Hardy: Yes. It's been misguided. Misguided by me. I thought I was right and now I think I was wrong. It can happen to anybody. Admitting it, that's the hard bit.

Heather: It has been suggested that large amounts of public money have been wasted.

Hardy: Yes. Millions. All my fault.

Heather: That's a rather devastating admission.

Hardy: It's only devastating because I admit it. Other people waste millions of pounds and don't get found out.

Heather: Who, for example?

Hardy: People who make bombs . . . . The War Office or the Bomb Office . . . it's a waste of money spending millions on bombs unless you drop them on somebody . . . and if you *do* drop them it's a waste of people and that's worse, wouldn't you say, sir? Madam? [**Gillian** *giggles*]

Heather: And what about your plans for the future, Mr Hardy?

Hardy: I shall feed the ducks. I may divine some water. I might make a baby, a brand new one . . . . [**Gillian** *giggles and holds up the sign reading: 'That which gives our dreams their daring is that they* can *be realized'*] Yes, that's it. I shall dream some daring dreams and one day I shall realize one of them . . . finding water in the desert, that would be a fair sort of dream to realize . . . .

Gillian: Just like life, wouldn't you say, Carstairs?

[*She and* **Hardy** *laugh out loud*]

Heather: Mr Hardy, thank you very much . . . .

Hardy: Aren't you going to let us choose a record?

Gillian: I bet if we were celebrating our golden wedding we could choose a record . . . .

Heather: What record did you want to hear?

Gillian: Eine Kleine Nachtmusik . . . .

Hardy: [*Simultaneously with* **Gillian**] Miles Davis . . .

Heather: That's two records.

Hardy: Compromise. Delius.

Gillian: Walk through the Paradise Garden.

Heather: Mr Hardy, thank you very much [**Hardy** *switches off the tape recorder*]

24 The 'All Saints' area

Hardy *is walking through the All Saints area – roughly the same route as he followed earlier but now he is dressed more casually: no tie, jeans, shirt, sweater. He finds his way to the pub and goes in.*

25 The pub

Hardy *enters.* **Beattie** *and* **Nell** *are in their usual places.*

Hardy: Afternoon . . . .

Beattie: Shh!

[*They are listening to* **Hardy** *being interviewed on the radio. We listen to the last bit with them*]

Hardy: [*On radio*] I shall dream some daring dreams

and one day I shall realize one of them . . . finding water in the desert, that would be a fair sort of dream to realize . . . .

Heather: [*On radio*] Mr Hardy, thank you very much.

Announcer: [*On radio*] Now for the weather forecast . . . .

Beattie: [*Switching off the radio*] What do you think of that, then?

Nell: Bloody idiot.

Hardy: I quite agree.

Nell: Lucky to have a job in the first place.

Beattie: Fancy packing it in.

Hardy: Don't you think it'll make any difference?

Beattie: Any difference to what?

Hardy: It might delay the bulldozer . . . or stop them altogether . . . top man resigning . . . .

Nell: [*With a nod towards the radio*] Is he a top man?

Hardy: Yes.

Nell: God help us!

Beattie: Wonder what the bottom men are like . . . .

Nell: Anyroad, it's all too late . . . . Haven't seen a Norwegian round here for ages . . . .

Beattie: The flowers have all withered and died, love . . . .

Hardy: There's you two.

Beattie: Crawler.

Hardy: Yes. Will you have a drink? I've got my redundancy money to spend . . . .

Beattie: You as well?

Hardy: On society's scrap heap . . . .

Nell: Have a drink with anybody, won't we?

Beattie: Why not?

Nell: The usual.

Beattie: Me an' all.

Hardy: Usuals all round. But a pint for me. I'm not driving.

Beattie: What happened to the big posh car?

Nell: And the big posh suit?

Hardy: Gave the car back to the boss. Left the suit hanging up somewhere.

Beattie: [*Pulls a pint for* **Hardy** *and pours two shorts for her and* **Nell**] There you are, Petal.

Hardy: Petal?

Beattie: If we are flowers, you can be a petal . . . it's only fair . . . . [*They take their drinks*]

Nell: It's months since anybody bought me a drink.

Beattie: Thank you.

Nell: Thank you.

Hardy: You're welcome. Cheers. [*They drink*]

Nell: Good health.

Beattie: Many of them [*Pause*] They know nothing, them fellers in the Town Hall.

Nell: Nothing.

Hardy: What makes you say that?

Nell: They're fellers.

Beattie: And they're in the Town Hall. So it stands to reason. [*Pause*]

Hardy: I'm not being rude but . . . what do you know?

[*They both laugh*]

Nell: What do we know?

Beattie: Nothing.

Nell: Me neither. Not a thing. Never have. Never will.

Beattie: But we admit it. We own up.

Hardy: I'll drink to that. [*And he does*]

26   The 'All Saints' area

Hardy *is making his way to* **Dan** *the barber's, but now he is in his new-look scruffy clothes. He walks into the barber's shop.*

27   The barber's shop.

Dan *looks up from his newspaper as* **Hardy** *comes in.*

Dan: Now then.

Hardy: Now then.

Dan: You're the feller that came in the other day.

Hardy: That's right.

Dan: You were looking for the way to somewhere . . . .

Hardy: No. You thought I was looking for the way to somewhere. You gave me a very good shave.

Dan: I *know* what I thought.

Hardy: Did you want to tell me the way again?

Dan: Not particularly. Where do you want to go?

Hardy: You decide.

Dan: Makes no odds. I tell everybody the same. Head down. Follow your nose. Dead reckoning.

Hardy: You could end up anywhere.

Dan: Aye, well, that's half the fun. If you want to go anywhere, that is. Me, I'd like to stay here. If they'd let me.

[*Pause*]

Hardy: How about a haircut?

Dan: I don't do light trims.

Hardy: Doesn't matter. I'm meeting my daughter . . . we're going to feed the ducks. I want to look smart. [*He crosses to the chair and sits down*] How about a short back and sides?

Dan: Hair cream and the lot?

Hardy: [*He ponders this*] Yes. Let's make lots of exciting new friends.

Dan: [*Preparing his equipment*] Aye, well, you'll have to if you're going to make that baby you were talking about on the wireless . . . .

[**Hardy** *is surprised: this is the first moment that* **Dan** *reveals that he knows who* **Hardy** *is*]

28 The 'All Saints' area

Hardy *emerges from* **Dan's** *shop – his hair cropped and plastered. There is a shriek of laughter from* **Gillian** *as she approaches.*

Gillian: What's that?

Hardy: Never mind what it is. It'll last till Christmas. [*They walk along, past a building on which is painted: 'Another fine mess – Hardy must go!'.* **Hardy** *and* **Gillian** *stop and look at it*] I went, didn't I?

Gillian: A very gallant gentleman.

Hardy: Very.

[*Pause*]

Gillian: That's your writing, isn't it?

Hardy: Yes.

29   A park

Ducks are swimming in a pond and bobbing about for bread, which is being thrown by **Hardy** *and* **Gillian**.

Hardy: Can you understand what they're saying?

Gillian: They're saying . . . a little late but very welcome . . . .

[*Pause*]

Hardy: This must be the only duck pond for twenty miles around.

Gillian: So . . . ?

30   The urban motorway complex

The same setting as the opening sequence. **Hardy** *and* **Gillian** *stand on the 'overpass'.*

Hardy: And when my daughter says 'What did you do to make the world a better place?' I shall say: 'Sweetheart – I made this!'

Gillian: But you didn't make that. [*She indicates a stretch of motorway under construction with earth-moving equipment busy among the mud*]

Hardy: Right. I didn't make that. [*Pause*] Let's go

and dig a well. [*They turn and walk away from the camera, with a hop and a skip and a defiant funny walk*]

The end

Follow-up Activities

Discussion
Lies
1 Why is Sammy critical of Rolo's shop-lifting?
2 Is Sammy a likeable character? Is he just a 'goodie-goodie'?
3 Is Mrs Stubbs a good mother? What can she be blamed for? What can be said in her defence?
4 Is Mr Derbyshire to blame for Sammy's disappointment about the warehouse? Or is it Sammy's own fault?
5 Is it a more serious crime to steal a car and to drive it away than to steal from a shop? Why?
6 What will happen to Sammy and Rolo when they return, do you think? What might happen to each of them over the next five years?
7 Why is the play called *Lies*? What lies are told during the course of the play?
8 Do you think it is possible for Sammy to create a better life for his family?

Uncle Sangi
9 Do you think Mr Dev is always as 'fair' as he claims to be?
10 Why does the neighbour behave as he does? Is he to

blame for the dog biting him? What do you think of
people like the neighbour?

11   What are Mr Dev's reasons for deciding that the
dog must be killed? Did it have to be put down?

12   Why did Uncle Sangi shoot his own dog? Why does
Sharm shoot his?

13   What advice would you give to someone who felt
isolated or lonely because of their race?

14   What do you think should be the law on immigration?

Short Back and Sides
15   What meanings does the play's title have?

16   Why does Hardy resign from his job? Will his
resignation have any effect?

17   Is he irresponsible? Does he care what he says?
Or what he does?

18   How do the various characters react to his resignation? Why are they not more pleased about it?

19   Were older types of inner city housing better than
modern blocks?

20   Would cities be better without private transport
and motorways or are both necessary?

21   What kind of housing and what amenities do city-
dwellers require?

22   How should we rebuild decaying city centres?

General
23   Do you find city life attractive? In what ways?
What are its drawbacks so far as you are concerned? How can a city 'trap' an individual?

24   'In the city, you live for the country; in the country
you praise the city.' Is this true?

25   Do you think these plays present a fair and true
picture of city life?

26 What do you think can be done to ease racial tension?
27 'That which gives our dreams their daring is that they *can* be realized.' What does Hardy mean by this statement (in *Short Back and Sides*, page 127)? Do you think it is true? Is it true for him? For Sammy (in *Lies*)?
28 Has a television play ever changed your ideas about a particular subject? In what way?

Drama

1 Improvise a scene in which someone who lives in the country talks about the attractions of city life to a city-dweller (like Sammy in *Lies*); the city-dweller then points out the disadvantages and describes his or her longing for a life in the country.
2 Improvise the scene that might take place at the Stubbs's house when Sammy returns home after stealing the car.
3 Improvise the scene that might take place when Sharm returns home after shooting his dog.
4 Improvise a scene in which a family discuss whether their pet (which is becoming a nuisance to the neighbours) should be put down.
5 Improvise a scene between a teenager (who is being teased or ignored because of his or her race) and the teenager's parents. (This could be about foreigners in this country or about people of your race abroad.)
6 Imagine a local council is planning to redevelop an area of your town. Improvise some of the planning sessions, a public meeting at which the planners explain their scheme to the local inhabitants, and subsequent meetings in which the inhabitants express their reactions. (You could develop these improvisations into a scripted play about city or

urban life in your locality.)

7 Adapt part of one of the scripts in this book to make a short, self-contained stage play. (See pages 20–22)

8 Present your own programme of short plays on the theme of 'city life'.

Writing

1 Write about a time when you have had to look after an adult, when you have tried to cheer up an adult, or when you have felt 'stronger' than someone older than yourself.

2 Write about a time you have felt badly let down by an adult (as Sammy feels he has been in *Lies*, and as Sharm feels in *Uncle Sangi*).

3 Write a short story called *The Truant*.

4 Describe part of a city you know well. Try to give your reader a sense of what it is like to walk through the area, or to 'belong' to that part of town.

5 Suppose the teacher in *Lies* were to write a report on the case of Sammy Stubbs. What might he say? Write his report. Write the report the policeman might have written on the case of the Devs, their dog and their neighbour. Or write the report that Carstairs might have written about his boss and the events leading up to his resignation.

6 Describe and illustrate with plans an ideal neighbourhood in an inner city area.

7 Write additional scenes that might take place after each of these plays has ended, involving the same characters.

8 Retell the events of one of the plays as a short story.

9 Write your own short stage or television play. Aim at presenting a short, clearly defined period of one person's life, and include only those characters who

are directly involved. Limit the number of settings – especially if you hope to stage the play.

Criticism

1 *Short Back and Sides* required six studio 'sets': Hardy's office, the lecture room, the local radio studio, the pub interior, the barber's shop interior and the living room of Hardy's house. It also required outdoor filming on three locations: the urban motorway complex, the 'All Saints' area (including the exterior of the pub and barber's shop) and the park. Try working out what studio sets and what location filming were required for *Lies* and for *Uncle Sangi*.

2 Do you like a play to be realistic? Which of the plays in this book do you find most convincing?

3 Which do you find most moving? Why? Which do you prefer? Why?

4 What weak points do some television plays have, so far as you are concerned?

5 Collect together a number of reviews of a television play you have seen recently, from a variety of papers. Which do you think are fair? Try reviewing another play (or one of the plays in this book).

6 Some newspapers 'preview' forthcoming programmes. With the help of *Radio Times* and *T V Times*, try writing a preview of a forthcoming television play, making your own judgements on whether you would recommend the play to other viewers.